GOOSE GREEN
1982

GOOSE GREEN
1982

GREGORY FREMONT-BARNES

DUNDURN
TORONTO

Author's note: All times refer to Falklands local time, which in April–June 1982 was four hours behind 'Zulu' time (GMT), used by officials in London.

Publisher's note: Unless otherwise credited, images are courtesy of Airborne Assault, The Museum of the Parachute Regiment and Airborne Forces, Duxford – we are enormously grateful for their help and kindness in allowing us to reproduce these photographs.

First published by Spellmount, an imprint of The History Press, 2013

Gregory Fremont-Barnes has asserted his moral right to be identified as the author of this work.

Printed in India

North American edition published by Dundurn Press, 2016

ISBN 978 1 4597 3393 0
A Cataloguing-in-Publication record for this book is available from Library and Archives Canada.

This book is also available in electronic formats: ISBN 978 1 4597 3394 7 (pdf); ISBN 978 1 4597 3395 4 (e-pub).

Care has been taken to trace the ownership of copyright material used in this book. The author and the publisher welcome any information enabling them to rectify any references in subsequent editions.
— J. Kirk Howard, President

Visit us at
Dundurn.com | @dundurnpress | Facebook.com/dundurnpress
Pinterest/dundurnpress

Dundurn
3 Church Street, Suite 500
Toronto, Ontario, Canada
M5E 1M2

CONTENTS

INTRODUCTION

Goose Green was the first and the longest battle of the Falklands War. It represented a fourteen-hour struggle with The Second Battalion the Parachute Regiment (2 Para) pitted against various sub-units of the Argentine army and air force over nearly featureless, wind-swept and boggy ground, most of it in clear daylight and against entrenched defenders. 2 Para were heavily outnumbered and lacked proper fire support; by all calculations they should have lost. In the event, they not only succeeded, but captured or killed the entire Argentine garrison – a force more than twice their size – and so set the tone for the engagements that were to follow in the drive against Stanley, the capital of the Falklands.

The battle is notable for a number of features. It was fought within just a week of the British landings at San Carlos Water – at the western end of East Falkland, the larger of the two main islands – as a consequence of the political priorities set by the British government to seize the initiative and maintain the momentum of the attack from the outset of the campaign. In doing so, ministers overrode the judgement of the land forces commander, Brigadier (Brig.) Julian Thompson, who believed an attack south was unnecessary and a diversion to the main thrust of his offensive against Stanley, clear on the other side of the island. A victory at Darwin and Goose Green, the government

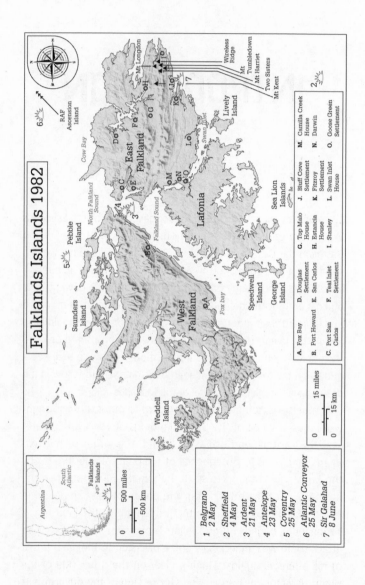

Falklands Islands 1982

A. Fox Bay
B. Port Howard
C. Port San Carlos
D. Douglas Settlement
E. San Carlos
F. Teal Inlet Settlement
G. Top Malo House
H. Estancia House
I. Stanley
J. Bluff Cove Settlement
K. Fitzroy Settlement
L. Swan Inlet House
M. Camilla Creek House
N. Darwin
O. Goose Green Settlement

1 Belgrano 2 May
2 Sheffield 4 May
3 Ardent 21 May
4 Antelope 23 May
5 Coventry 25 May
6 Atlantic Conveyor 25 May
7 Sir Galahad 8 June

Marines from 42 Commando disarm Argentine prisoners at Stanley, 14 June. (Ted Nevill)

and its strategists at Northwood and the Ministry of Defence in London concluded, would form a prelude to further attacks in the drive on the capital. In so doing, it would preserve the high degree of public support enjoyed at home and set a precedent for other successes on the battlefield to come.

Thus, Goose Green stands as an example of how political intervention can and does – for good or ill – interfere with military priorities set by commanders in the field. Thompson was quite right: the Argentines at Goose Green did not pose a threat to the beachhead established by the amphibious landings, and London made little attempt to establish this as a rationale for 2 Para's attack. So long as Thompson could prosecute his advance across the northern route to Stanley – an operation feasible by foot and by helicopter – the garrison at Goose Green could be pinned in place, exerting very little influence on events beyond the narrow isthmus upon which the tiny settlements of Darwin and Goose Green sit. Nor did the Argentines expect such an attack, which accounts for the peculiar composition of the forces deployed there.

The Battle of Goose Green may, nevertheless, be seen as a pivotal event in the Falklands War. By boosting the morale of British forces and, conversely, fatally damaging that of the Argentines, its result had a profound effect on both sides for the remainder of this brief, yet decisive, campaign. Victory at Goose Green established British forces' moral superiority over the defenders, a position which maintained the momentum of the ground offensive until the point of Argentine surrender on the Falklands as a whole, little more than two weeks later.

The battle is also noteworthy for the degree to which the attackers operated outside an all-arms context. When 2 Para struck on 28 May 1982, it did so largely unassisted, with the odds heavily against it. The battalion faced twice its numbers; the defenders occupied entrenched positions overlooking gently undulating, open ground, which they could sweep with rifle, machine-gun, mortar and artillery fire. The quality of 2 Para's highly trained, highly motivated personnel bore no resemblance to their opponents, but in light of 2 Para's almost complete lack of support from other arms, it found itself largely dependent on its own resources to cope against poor odds. This was exacerbated by the lack of air support until the close of the battle; only the briefest naval support; the absence of most of the battalion's heavy weapons until very late in the day; the absence of armoured support; and grossly inadequate artillery support. The battalion was left to fight its way through enemy defences with rifle, grenade, machine-gun, light anti-tank rockets and just two mortars. It took fourteen hours of close-quarter fighting to move 6km (3.7 miles), some of it in darkness. This, by any standard, stands as a remarkable achievement.

The fact that Goose Green need never have been fought in order for British forces to attain their objective – defeating the main concentration of Argentine forces in and around Stanley – must not detract from the battle's significance. Having made the decision to engage the Argentine garrison there, a great deal hinged on the outcome of the engagement – particularly if Britain had lost. The British were off to an auspicious start a week before Goose Green, when 3 Commando Brigade, of which 2 Para constituted but one of five battalions, had effected a successful lodgement and secured a bridgehead against possible counter-attack. But victory was by no means inevitable, for at the same time Royal Navy ships just offshore found themselves under intense air attack and suffered accordingly high losses: four ships destroyed and five seriously damaged in the week of the landings. If to these losses were added a defeat inflicted against 2 Para, it is difficult to underestimate the negative repercussions that would have occurred back in Britain, both in Whitehall and amongst the public at large.

Quite apart from the serious impact on the morale of the armed forces in theatre, a repulse of 2 Para would result in a delayed offensive against Stanley, and time was in woefully short supply. Even if the simultaneous movement east of ground forces proceeded as planned (and there would have been a real prospect that, in the wake of a defeat at Goose Green, this offensive would be cancelled

Argentine prisoners. In all, 13,000 fell into British hands during the course of the war.

2 Para's flag flying over Goose Green after the settlement's liberation on 29 May. (Dr Stephen Hughes)

altogether with forces digging in around Ajax Bay in a defensive posture) it was more than likely that the Argentines, elated by success at Goose Green, would launch a counter-thrust against the meagre British forces, 3 Para and 45 Commando Royal Marines, already en route to Mount Kent on foot. True, reinforcements were on their way to the Falklands in the form of 5 Infantry Brigade, but the delay forced upon Thompson would have derailed his timetable – a timetable utterly dependent upon taking Stanley before the full weight of winter brought a swift halt to any British offensive. Ships could not operate in the rough seas of the South Atlantic winter; aircraft could not fly combat sorties, or helicopters ferry troops and supplies or evacuate the wounded; logistics would break down; and the troops, exposed to snow and freezing winds, would find themselves huddled in a ring around San Carlos and unable to move or, worse still, obliged to disembark. This, in turn, would have forced the Task Force to Ascension Island 6,500km away or, more probably, home to lick its wounds and reflect on its failure to liberate the Falklands.

In the event, the Argentines surrendered on 14 June – with no time to spare for the Task Force. In this respect, the outcome of the fighting at Goose Green may rightly be seen to assume a position of vital importance to the war itself.

TIMELINE

Goose Green 1982

1982

5 April	First elements of the Task Force sail from Portsmouth, including 3 Para aboard the requisitioned P&O liner *Canberra*
11–16 April	Reacting to the dispatch of the Task Force from the UK, Argentines reinforce the islands by air with 9 Brigade under Brigadier General Oscar Jofre, Land Forces Commander, himself under Brigadier General Mario Menendez, Commander-in-Chief and governor of Las Malvinas
12 April	Britain declares a 200-mile Maritime Exclusion Zone (MEZ) around the Falkland Islands
16 April	Task force proceeds south from Ascension Island, approximately 6,500km from the Falklands
22 April	Senior Argentine commanders meet to devise defensive strategy to prevent Task Force re-establishing British control over the Falklands
25 April	Brigadier General Omar Parada, Commander of 3 Brigade (West Falkland and the western half of East Falkland), posts 12th Regiment under Lieutenant Colonel Italo Piaggi to Goose Green, reinforcing the small garrison already there
26 April	Argentine commander on South Georgia surrenders to a company of Royal Marines landed to retake the island. Second Battalion the Parachute Regiment sails from Hull aboard the North Sea passenger ferry *Norland*
28 April	Britain announces Total Exclusion Zone (TEZ) around the Falklands to include aircraft and ships of all nations
30 April	Main Task Force reaches TEZ
May	Piaggi lays mines at various points on the Darwin-Goose Green isthmus, particularly near the beaches
1 May	Royal Air Force (RAF) Vulcan bomber strikes Stanley airfield, but with limited results

14

Timeline

1982

2 May	Nuclear submarine HMS *Conqueror* sinks the Argentine cruiser *General Belgrano*
4 May	Argentine Exocet missile, fired from an aircraft, strikes HMS *Sheffield*, causing her to sink six days later
6 May	2 Para arrives at Ascension Island
7 May	Main body of amphibious task group leaves Ascension Island
12 May	The requisitioned luxury liner *Queen Elizabeth II* sails from Southampton with 5 Infantry Brigade
14–15 May	A squadron of the Special Air Service (SAS) raids Pebble Island, destroying eleven Argentine aircraft on the ground
	As a precaution in the event of attack, Piaggi concentrates all 114 residents of Darwin and Goose Green in the latter settlement's community hall
21 May	Amphibious landings made at 0430 hrs by 3 Commando Brigade, consisting of 2 and 3 Para, and 40, 42 and 45 Commando RM, in San Carlos Water. HMS *Ardent* sunk by aircraft, signifying the beginning of six days of regular air attacks on British vessels in Falkland Sound
	2 Para leaves the beachhead and advances south to Sussex Mountain, establishing itself on the summit around 0630 hrs; SAS launch diversionary raid against Argentine position near Darwin
22 May	3 Commando Brigade established ashore at Ajax Bay, with Rapier anti-aircraft batteries in place and a defensive perimeter around the beachhead. Thompson meets with Lieutenant Colonel 'H' Jones, Commanding Officer of 2 Para, and orders him to conduct a raid against Goose Green
23 May	HMS *Antelope* sunk

1982

23–24 May	Jones draws up plan for raid against Darwin-Goose Green
25 May	HMS *Coventry* sunk. More critically, when the transport vessel *Atlantic Conveyor* is mortally damaged by an Exocet on the same day, the Task Force loses all ten helicopters on board, causing a transport and logistics crisis for Thompson. At nightfall, 2 Para begins its march to Camilla Creek House, designated as the start line for the raid, but Thompson cancels the operation and troops return to Sussex Mountain
26 May	Northwood resurrects plan for raid against Goose Green. Jones is elated
27 May	In the early hours, 2 Para leaves Sussex Mountain for the second time and advances to Camilla Creek House. At 1000 hrs, BBC World Service announces presence of a parachute unit poised to attack Goose Green; at 1500 hrs Jones assembles 'O' group and issues company orders consisting of a six-phase, silent/noisy, night/day battalion attack
	45 Commando and 3 Para commence 'yomp' and 'tab', respectively, from San Carlos to Mount Kent as preparation for assaults on ring of Argentine defences west of Stanley
28 May	Battle of Goose Green
29 May	Argentines surrender at Goose Green; over 1,200 prisoners taken
30 May	Major General Jeremy Moore arrives in the Falklands and replaces Thompson as land forces commander; Thompson resumes command over 3 Commando Brigade
31 May	42 Commando RM transported by air from San Carlos to Mount Kent, while 45 Commando reaches Teal Inlet on foot. 3 Para, also on foot, reaches Douglas Settlement

Timeline

1982

1 June	5 Brigade begins disembarking at San Carlos. 3 Commando Brigade forward HQ established at Teal Inlet
2 June	Helicopters ferry 2 Para to Bluff Cove in the south of the island
5 June	Scots Guards embark for Fitzroy aboard *Sir Tristram*
6 June	Welsh Guards embark for Fitzroy in HMS *Fearless* but ship withheld. Scots Guards land at Fitzroy, where 5 Brigade establishes forward base
8 June	Argentine aircraft bomb *Sir Galahad* and *Sir Tristram* at Fitzroy, killing dozens of Welsh Guardsmen and sailors. Moore finalises plans for final offensive against defenders dug in west of Stanley
11–12 June	Thompson launches three simultaneous battalion-sized attacks against Mount Longdon, Mount Harriet and Two Sisters
12–13 June	Two further simultaneous attacks, against Mount Tumbledown and Wireless Ridge
14 June	Argentine forces in the Falklands surrender to General Moore, bringing a close to the fighting as weather conditions continue to worsen and British supplies near exhaustion
20 June	In the final operation of the war, part of M Company, 42 Commando, Royal Marines accepts the surrender of Argentine garrison on the remote island of South Thule, South Sandwich Islands, 2,000km (1,240 miles) south-east of the Falklands

HISTORICAL BACKGROUND:
WHAT WERE THEY FIGHTING FOR?

The Falkland Islands are situated deep in the South Atlantic, 13,000km from Britain and approximately 650km from Argentina. In 1982 the islands were – and continue to be – the subject of a territorial dispute between the two countries. The dispute formally dates from 1833, but rests on a complex chain of events which preceded that year. In 1540, the islands appear to have formed a refuge for several months for the crew of a Spanish ship that survived a violent gale in the Straits of Magellan. The crew made no claim on behalf of Spain and did not leave a settlement behind. Half a century later, in 1592, the islands may have been sighted by the British vessel *Desire*, but there is no solid evidence of the authenticity of this claim and no landing appears to have been made at the time. A Dutch ship is confirmed to have sighted outlying islands of the Falklands two years later, but again, no settlers remained behind to establish a claim. The first confirmed British connection took place in 1690, when Captain (Capt.) John Strong, sailing the *Welfare* out of Plymouth, sighted land and sailed along the passage between the two main islands, naming this body of water Falkland Sound, in honour of Viscount Falkland, the First Lord of the Admiralty. Yet again, no one remained behind, leaving the place for the use of French seal-hunters, who from 1698 regularly landed there and named the islands Les Iles Malouines in honour of St Malo, their home port in Brittany. The Spanish subsequently altered the name to Las Malvinas, the title since adopted by the Argentines.

Actual settlement of the islands dates from 1764, when the French established a presence on Port Louis, East Falkland in an effort to colonise the islands as a whole. The following year Capt. John Byron, on behalf of the British government, landed on West Falkland at a place he dubbed Port Egmont, 130km (80 miles) from the French settlement, proclaiming both islands and the many hundreds of smaller ones around them on behalf of his sovereign – although he left behind no one to furnish substance to his claim. In 1766, another British captain landed a hundred settlers at Port Egmont, almost certainly unaware of the existence of the French settlement at Port Louis, although a short time later a British ship encountered the post and informed the inhabitants of their rival claim. Events became more complex the following year when, upon becoming aware of the existence of Port Louis, the Spanish disputed the French right to occupy what Madrid regarded as its territory. They did so on the grounds that the islands formed an offshore dependency of its mainland colony, the Royalty of La Plata, which included all of modern-day Argentina and considerably more territory besides. The French agreed to evacuate the islands in return for financial compensation, so enabling the Spanish to replace the garrison with one of their own, together with a governor at Puerto Soledad, their new name for Port Louis.

Two years later, in 1769, a Spanish ship sighted Port Egmont while sailing in Falkland Sound, in consequence of which six Spanish ships carrying 1,400 troops arrived at this tiny post the following year and forced the British to evacuate it. In 1771, after threatening to send a naval expedition to retake their post and establish their claim over the islands by force, the British obtained Spain's acquiescence in restoring Port Egmont, but Madrid insisted that, in doing so, it did not relinquish its overall sovereignty of the islands. Owing to the excessive expense of maintaining its presence at so great a distance, the British removed their settlement from Port Egmont in 1774, leaving behind a plaque laying claim to the whole of the Falkland Islands.

Meanwhile, at Puerto Soledad on East Falkland, a succession of Spanish governors served at their respective posts down to 1811, in which year, owing to the end of Spanish rule over La Plata, the Spanish settlements withdrew, leaving the islands unoccupied until 1826. In the meantime, however, Argentina had emerged as an independent state in 1816 and, as a result of its perceived inheritance of Spain's former territories, claimed the Falklands at least as early as 1820, when a ship arrived. They did not, however, establish a permanent settlement. This soon changed when, in 1826, the Argentines established a settlement at Puerto Soledad, posting Louis Vernet as governor. London sent its protests to Buenos Aires but took no military action. Five years later, the American government sent the warship *Lexington*, under Capt. Silas Duncan, to remove Vernet on grounds that the Argentines had employed force in denying American sealers access to the islands. The American government made no claim and, in 1832, Argentina dispatched a new governor, Major (Maj.) Mestivier, to the islands. Unrest amongst his men arose, however, and in the process of their mutiny the men murdered Mestivier. In 1833 Buenos Aires sent another governor to restore order, but during the course of his efforts to do so, Capt. John Onslow of HMS *Clio* arrived with a small force that evicted the Argentines, raised the Union flag and proclaimed the islands for King William IV. From this point on British settlers arrived, establishing themselves mainly at Stanley harbour, and inaugurating a period of sovereignty which remained disputed but physically unopposed until the Argentine invasion of 2 April 1982.

Since 1833 Argentina's claim has rested – and continues to rest – on the basis that upon independence from Spain, Argentina could rightfully claim her former territories, including Las Malvinas (the Falkland Islands). The foundation for such a claim has its regional precedents, too. Chile controls the Juan Fernández Islands, which

Point-detonating artillery rounds

When firing at an entrenched defender, it is usually preferable to delay the explosion of shells by a fraction of a second in order to allow the shell time to penetrate into the target – a simple process achieved by turning a small screw contained in the fuse. At Goose Green, however, the softness of the soil enabled PD ammunition to penetrate so easily that gun crews dispensed with time-delayed fuses. Indeed, the sogginess of the ground actually reduced the effectiveness of artillery fire, since the ground absorbed some of the impact of the explosions, limiting its effect. To those on the receiving end of artillery or mortar fire, therefore, the otherwise unpleasant soggy ground provided some advantage.

lie 650km (400 miles) offshore – not to mention Easter Island, which is situated 3,200km west, deep in the Pacific. Ecuador, another former Spanish colony, administers the Galapagos Islands, more than 1,000km away, and Brazil rules Trinidade Island, also over 1,000km offshore. The Argentines contend that the British used force to evict their governor in 1833 and then introduced settlers to confirm an illegal transfer of power. The fact that the British had controlled a small post on West Falkland, Argentina deemed irrelevant, as Port Egmont survived a mere five years, the British abandoning it decades before the Argentines began their own settlement of the islands in 1826, which itself came closely on the heels of a continuous period of Spanish control stretching from 1767 to 1811.

The British, for their part, assert that the arguments underpinning their claim to the islands hold greater merit, on the basis that Argentine control of the Falklands remained tenuous during the seven-year period preceding British arrival. Above all, they assert that since 1833 Britain has maintained a continuous, stable presence, with its inhabitants almost wholly of British descent, in many cases tracing their predecessors' residence

21

back five or more generations. From the British perspective, the principle of settling a claim of sovereignty stretching back more than a century and a half makes little sense in light of the fact that, if the same principle were applied across the world, virtually no nation would stand immune from territorial adjustment, sometimes radically so.

The problem, at length, rests with the definition of sovereignty. Argentina possesses a *de jure* claim to this principle dating back a considerable period, whereas Britain's *de facto* position of sovereignty lends a degree of credibility to her case. Nor does the complexity of the issue stop there, for the Falklands include the dependencies of South Georgia, the South Sandwich Islands and, significantly, all modern British governors based at Stanley have been invested with authority over the British Antarctic Territory as well. South Georgia is 3,750 square km of glacier and mountain, which lies 2,000km from the South American mainland. Although a seemingly worthless piece of territory, it was important for whalers for generations and has been the site of a British scientific research station since 1909. Moreover, Argentina's claim only dates from 1927. The South Sandwich Islands lie 750km south-east of South Georgia and consist of a chain of volcanic islands measuring 240km long, discovered by Captain Cook in 1775 during his voyage en route to the Pacific. Conditions amongst these very isolated islands are Antarctic; characterised by permanent ice and strong, freezing winds. They are uninhabited and, perhaps as important, uninhabitable. Apart from Argentina's unauthorised establishment of a 'scientific' base on Cook Island from 1964 to 1982, the islands have never been occupied. Finally, control of at least a portion of Antarctica rounds off the whole, complicated issue of sovereignty across a large swathe of the South Atlantic. While various nations with interests in Antarctica, including Argentina, Britain and Chile (all of whom dispute the same area of that frozen continent) have by international agreement dating from 1961 consented to hold their territorial claims in abeyance, the fact remains that a British scientific presence has existed for decades and successive British governments have refused to establish any precedent whereby recognition of Argentine claims to the Falklands can be construed to extend to the British Antarctic Territory.

Argentina's claim over the Falkland Island dependencies led, in 1947, to Britain putting its case before the International Court of Justice at The Hague, but Argentina refused this arbitration. When Britain unilaterally submitted its case in 1955, the court agreed to consider the dispute, but when Argentina announced its refusal to comply with any decision reached, officials closed proceedings the following year. In 1960, however, Argentina believed it had a strong case on the basis of the United Nations (UN) General Assembly's new policy designed to encourage self-determination; specifically, to render independent the numerous colonies, particularly those in Africa, still under white rule. Yet the Falklands stood in a unique position, for the UN declaration did not take into account – much to Argentina's dismay – the peculiar situation of the Islanders, who were themselves white, maintained a democratically elected local government in Stanley, and wished to maintain their colonial relationship with Britain. In short, the wording of the new UN declaration, while applicable across much of the world, did not meet the criteria of a largely self-governing people who desired to preserve their connection with its mother country. 'All peoples,' the document read,

… have the right to self-determination; by virtue of that right they freely determine their political status and freely pursue their economic, social and cultural development … Immediate steps shall be taken, in trust and non-self-government territories or all other territories which have not yet attained independence, to transfer all powers to the peoples of those territories, without any conditions or reservations, in accordance with their freely expressed will and desire, without any distinction as to race, creed or color, in order to enable them to enjoy complete independence and freedom.

The dilemma created by this statement left the UN only able to issue a vaguely worded resolution in 1965, which invited the British and Argentine governments to open negotiations based on the aspirations stated in the declaration, in order to find a peaceful solution to the dispute. Apart from a few abstentions, including Britain's, ninety-four nations in the General Assembly voted in favour of the resolution, but its wording was sufficiently unclear on the principle of sovereignty as to leave Argentina frustrated that her claim over the Falkland Islands remained tenuous. In such peculiar circumstances, the principle of self-determination – whether or not in tandem with sovereignty, however defined – operated effectively and to the satisfaction of those who wished to retain their connection with the mother country.

Talks nonetheless began in 1966, but with no result. Even if successive British governments wanted to separate the link with the Falklands owing to the damage the issue was causing for trade and diplomatic relations across South America (and evidence of this emerged all the way up to 1982), the fact remained that they could not do so as long as the islanders themselves expressed a desire to remain a UK Overseas Territory; that is to say, effectively self-governing except insofar as its trade, defence and foreign relations were concerned. Besides, notwithstanding the disadvantages arising out of the dispute, Britain continued to maintain an interest in the South Atlantic quite apart from the Falklands themselves, long before engineers discovered large oil reserves beneath the sea floor – reserves which still remain unexploited. Moreover, no joint control proved feasible since neither the islanders nor the Argentines were prepared to reach a compromise. Appeals to the wider world from Buenos Aires counted for little, since most people could appreciate that exchanging Argentine for British sovereignty would merely result in the deeply unpopular control of one group over another – in precise contradiction to the UN 'Declaration on the Granting of Independence to Colonial Countries and Peoples' of 1960. Besides, so long as open hostilities did not occur – especially those which might potentially involve repercussions elsewhere – the dispute remained practically unrecognised by everyone except the parties immediately concerned. Talks between London and Buenos Aires concluded only two months before the Argentine invasion in April 1982, with no progress.

If in international law nations increasingly gave credence to the principle of self-determination over sovereignty, then the arguments seemed, by 1982, to be favouring Britain. However, the Thatcher government did little to develop an impression in the minds of Argentine military and political leaders that Britain stood determined to hold on to the Falklands, irrespective of Argentine demands. Not only did the British government do little to bolster its claim with a clear policy, a number of circumstances in fact probably went far in persuading the Argentines that Britain was gradually withdrawing its interests in the South Atlantic, thus inadvertently encouraging Buenos Aires to cease its hitherto frustrated diplomatic initiatives and choose a military option. Since the 1950s, for instance, the British garrison in the Falklands consisted of one naval party, which in 1982 totalled a mere forty-two Royal Marines, plus the ice patrol vessel HMS *Endurance*, the only ship the Royal Navy regularly deployed in South Atlantic waters. Neither the British Army nor the Royal Air Force possessed any assets in the area, and the closest British forces beyond the Falklands garrison were stationed in Belize, the former colony of British Honduras, almost 8,000km (5,000 miles) away. The Argentines occasionally made naval demonstrations in the area, prompting the government of James Callaghan in 1977 to dispatch a submarine and a few surface vessels, but these maintained a distant station, undetected by the Argentines, and no substantial naval presence remained to monitor Argentine activity.

Under Margaret Thatcher's premiership, further signs developed which, quite erroneously, indicated to Argentina that Britain would not resist armed intervention. When, in 1981, the helicopter aboard *Endurance* sighted the Argentine base in the South Sandwich Islands and recognised that the size of

THE PARAS

The Paras ranked amongst the best of Britain's armed forces. Unlike the Royal Marines Commandos in 3 Commando Brigade, they were not specifically trained in winter warfare; indeed, they were imminently due for jungle training in Belize when war broke out. However, they could operate in practically any environment. Put simply, a paratrooper could march faster, entrench himself more effectively and shoot more accurately than his Argentine counterpart, who displayed a much lower standard of marksmanship, fieldcraft and general discipline. The Paras were entirely volunteers, often with many years' professional experience, National Service in Britain having been abolished twenty years before. This fact alone rendered 2 Para innately superior to the defenders at Darwin and Goose Green. Argentina's decision to leave their best troops behind in case of hostilities with Chile proved a costly mistake.

the buildings exceeded the needs of the scientific community, which Buenos Aires insisted composed its only occupants, London rejected the captain's request to evict them. In the same year, when the British scientific station on South Georgia moved to a more modest building for the sake of cost-effective maintenance, the Argentines wrongly assumed this represented a greatly diminished financial investment in the area. When the British government postponed construction of new barracks for the Royal Marines' garrison on the Falklands, again the Argentines interpreted this as a sign of Whitehall's growing indifference to future British sovereignty over the region. Much more critically – and the significance of two further factors cannot be underestimated – the 1981 UK Defence Review under John Nott reached the conclusion that, rather than replace the veteran *Endurance*, she should be decommissioned after completing her tour of duty, leaving no Royal Naval presence in

South Atlantic waters at all. Further, in the same year, by a single vote the House of Lords refused to grant full rights of residence to Falkland Islanders – a privileged status already extended to residents of Gibraltar. Unsurprisingly, Buenos Aires attached much significance to these developments, a circumstance that was reinforced when, at the failed UN talks in February 1982, only two months before the invasion, the British delegation issued no firm statement declaring the Thatcher government's resolve to oppose any aggressive moves by Argentina to enforce her claim over the islands.

Moreover, Argentina's growing relationship with the islanders themselves almost certainly encouraged the impression in Buenos Aires that the connection with their neighbour was not altogether unwelcome. Indeed, even as diplomatic sparring continued, the islanders sustained their decade-long agreement with LADE (Líneas Aéreas del Estado), a commercial airline run by the Argentine Air Force that operated bi-weekly flights to the mainland; they made use of an Argentine maritime freight service; permitted the maintenance of storage facilities for petrol, bottled gas and oil supplied by Argentine companies; and enjoyed the benefits of obtaining medical services from Argentina for patients requiring more resources than the islands could supply. Not only did employees from the airline and the fuel companies reside amicably in Stanley, but Falklands school children received instruction in Spanish from teachers recruited from the mainland. In short, while the islanders certainly expressed no interest in Argentine rule, the general trend in relations suggested advantages in strengthening connections with the mainland.

All these factors, together with hyper-inflation in Argentina and growing public disillusionment with the deeply unpopular, highly repressive junta under General (Gen.) Galtieri – whose regime consequently sought to distract opposition by galvanising opinion around a highly emotive issue such as Las Malvinas – laid the basis for Argentina's invasion in the spring of 1982.

THE ARMIES

Argentine Forces

In 1982 the Argentine army numbered approximately 60,000 troops, which compared favourably with other South American forces. The brigade functioned as the principal operational unit, each performing a specialised function according to its type: armoured, mechanised, infantry, mountain, jungle and airmobile. Argentine infantry regiments consisted of approximately 550–650 officers and men, divided amongst several companies, but of which only three consisted of 'rifle' companies tasked with conducting most of the fighting. Each company in turn was divided into three platoons, often including support weapons like heavy machine-guns. Platoons tended to be organised on the American model, with their squads (the equivalent of a British section, or half-platoon) led by sergeants. Officers and newly commissioned officers (NCOs) were professionals; careerists who trained and led conscripted soldiers serving a year of military service, which commenced when they turned 19.

Since the training cycle began in January, with whole regiments bringing in new recruits for training, most units were only just into their fourth month of training when they received orders to pack their kit and board aircraft. They were to reinforce the amphibious

Argentine soldier

Argentine rank and file wore a padded, hooked parka with a zipped front, and knitted cuffs, American-issue steel helmet, olive drab fatigues and high black combat boots, the typical Argentine soldier carried an equipment harness (in British parlance, 'webbing') usually of grey-green leather, a bayonet frogged on the left hip, a canteen, and a small pack on the right hip. Leather gloves were used extensively, together with a field cap with pile-lined flaps. In addition, he carried the light 'assault pack', to which he attached a blanket and a spade thrust under the straps at the back. Alternatively, he carried a horse-shoe blanket rolled around his body. His rifle, unlike his British counterpart's, was automatic, and together with the excellent, widely issued optical equipment also available to the crews of the heavy .50 calibre heavy machine-gun, offered a degree of superiority over the attackers' Self-Loading Rifles (SLR) and General-Purpose Machine-Guns (GPMG). Nevertheless, many soldiers were mere raw recruits, and even reservists paled in terms of training, discipline and motivation against their opponents.

Argentine officers

Very little is known about the Argentine commanders who served in the Falklands, especially those below the rank of brigadier. At Goose Green, 1st Lt Estoban commanded C Company 25th Infantry Regiment, the bulk of that unit remaining at Stanley, 100km away. The son of an Air Force officer, Estoban was 27, and had graduated second in his class of 250 from the Army's academy. One of his subordinates, Lt Roberto Estevez – the only Argentine officer to die in the battle – served as a platoon commander in C Company. Officers were all professionals, most of whom deliberately remained aloof from other ranks, a characteristic which British personnel noted as one of the many features which served the Argentines ill during the campaign. Officers received better rations than their men, including alcohol, whereas meals served to British troops were identical for all ranks.

troops who overwhelmed the diminutive Royal Marine garrison based at Moody Brook Barracks, just west of Stanley, in the course of brief fighting on 2 April. The recruits can only be described as 'green' and had not yet even handled heavy weapons such as mortars, machine-guns or anti-tank guns – hence the importance of recalling reservists. Morale was generally poor, for although they enjoyed the benefit of adopting a defensive position, digging in proved extremely difficult owing to the thin layer of soil through which water rapidly penetrated, and beneath which a lower layer absorbed and retained the water. Trenches consequently became waterlogged, or even flooded when it rained. Frostbite and trench foot became common maladies, leading to the continuous loss of personnel through sickness. Still, from the comparative safety of his entrenched position – trench or bunker – at Goose Green, even the newest recruit was capable of mounting a creditable degree of resistance to an attacker.

Argentina did deploy marines and other elite units to the Falklands, but as they did not figure in the fighting at Goose Green they need not concern us here. The paucity of hardened troops in the islands was, in fact, to prove a grave error in Argentine strategic planning. In light of concerns of growing tensions with Chile over a long-standing territorial dispute involving the Beagle Channel – which runs through Tierra del Fuego at the southern-most point of the continent – the Argentines saw fit to retain their best troops for a scenario that envisaged a Chilean attack. Meanwhile, 13,000 Argentines dug in on the Falklands in anticipation of a possible British military response. If it was necessary that the bulk of Argentine forces remained at home, they did at least call up a large proportion of reservists – men who had left the ranks only the previous December when their term of service had expired. These, together with a leavening of officers and NCOs, characterised the ground units available for the defence of the isthmus on which sat the settlements of Darwin and Goose Green. Officers were traditionally drawn from wealthy families with a long tradition of supplying their sons to the military; NCOs were

Capt. Mark Worsley Tonks (who took over as adjutant of 2 Para), Lt Col David Chaundler, Maj. Chris Keeble, and Regimental Sergeant-Major (RSM) Simpson in front of a captured Argentine anti-aircraft gun. At Goose Green the defenders deployed four such weapons: two each of 35mm and 20mm guns.

also professionals, but a lack of education and their humbler social background denied them promotion to officer rank. The army, therefore, stood socially stratified, characterised by a wide social gulf between officers and other ranks.

Army and marine units on the Falklands had at their disposal armoured cars; 105mm and 155mm artillery; 20mm, 30mm and 35mm anti-aircraft guns; and Roland, Tigercat and Blowpipe surface-to-air missiles (SAMs), though most of these remained amongst the main garrison at or around Stanley, on the other side of East Falkland. Specifically, Argentine troops deployed at Goose Green possessed no armoured cars, no field guns except two pack howitzers, and no SAMs. They were, however, armed with light machine-guns, the American 3.5in rocket launcher fitted with a folding bipod, and as many as six rifle grenades per soldier. Air force personnel responsible for maintaining aircraft at the airfield

Brigadier General Mario Menendez

Brigadier General Mario Menendez was commander of all Argentine forces in the Falklands. Although in control of numerically superior forces, he laboured under the disadvantage of not knowing the site of the British landing or whether or not it would constitute the main effort or merely a diversion. Unable to disperse his troops everywhere, Menendez compromised by distributing them across the islands in key locations, with most concentrated around Stanley. He described the strategic problem thus: 'There was really no structured plan for the defence of the islands because the original plan for the occupation of the Malvinas did not contemplate the possibility of a British military reaction. Naturally this caused serious problems later on because we had to improvise a defence plan, and when other military units started arriving in the Malvinas sometimes they didn't have proper logistical support ... We tried to organize a defence as best we could.' (Adkin, *Goose Green*, p. 78)

General Menendez. (Ted Nevill)

at Goose Green deployed three anti-aircraft guns, which could help repel Harrier attack as well as operate against ground targets. The local commander could also call upon limited air support and helicopter-borne reinforcements. Very fortunately for their opponents, no jet fighters operated well in the islands owing to inadequate airstrips – and hence the regular raids conducted by Super Etendards and Mirages from the mainland 650km away. The Argentine air force could, however, operate Pucara aircraft locally out of Pebble Island, Goose Green and Stanley. The Pucaras best served in a counterinsurgency role, but constituted a particular menace to helicopters, of which the British maintained precious few. It had two seats, though the Argentines normally only supplied the pilot, who enjoyed excellent manoeuvrability, a speed of 78 knots and impressive firepower, including two 20mm cannons, four 7.62mm machine-guns, plus either air-to-ground missiles, napalm or bombs. The Argentines initially deployed a squadron of twelve Pucaras to Stanley as of 9 April, moving some of these to Goose Green on the 29th. Some of these propeller-driven light aircraft flew over Goose Green during the battle on

Argentine anti-aircraft gun. Four of these operated at Goose Green, largely in a ground role during 2 Para's advance against the flagpole position and the schoolhouse.

several occasions, taking off from the 450m-long grass airstrip controlled by air force personnel under Vice-Commodore Wilson Pedroza, whose anti-aircraft capability there consisted of two twin 35mm Oerlikon and six twin 20mm Rheinmetall guns.

British Forces

The Second Battalion The Parachute Regiment under Lieutenant Colonel (Lt Col) 'H' Jones formed the mainstay of the British force at Goose Green. The regiment as a whole consisted of three battalions, two of which served in the Falklands, with 3 Para distinguishing itself at Mount Longdon, two weeks after Goose Green. 2 Para had a strength of about 650, divided into several companies each led by majors, with each company divided into three platoons led by captains, themselves divided into sections led by corporals. These personnel, like all other components of the British Army and in sharp contrast to Argentine forces, consisted entirely of volunteers – all thoroughly professional and, specifically in the case of this elite battalion, highly trained, at the peak of physical fitness and exceptionally well motivated. Maj. Chris Keeble, second-in-command (2ic) at Goose Green, described his unit's unique bond:

> I was enormously attracted to the Parachute Regiment because of this wonderful feeling of comradeship. We all have to go through a traumatic selection process, which weeds out a great number of people. We are united in our hardship, by what we have done. It is a very good way of preparing for the actual trauma of war. Soldiers do not fight for Queen and country, or even for Maggie [Margaret Thatcher, the Prime Minister] – they fight for each other. But they need to know that their comrades would do the same. Selection produces that mutual trust.
>
> (Arthur, *Above All, Courage*, p. 191)

In a subsequent interview, he added:

… we are a body of people welded together by our traditions, by our regiment, by a feeling of togetherness. We're a family of people and you have to remember that. We all know each other, we know each other's families. This is a body of people who would die for each other … We have to win, the mission is paramount. It is more important than anything else.

(Adkin, *Goose Green*, p. 22)

2 Para wore camouflage of light green, yellow, light red-brown and black, and headgear consisting of either a helmet or their distinctive maroon beret with characteristic winged cap badge. They wore 'Northern Ireland' boots and sometimes over-boots or puttees, which were intended for use in central Europe rather than amidst the topography and climate of the South Atlantic. Indeed,

British paratroopers. At Goose Green these men wore lightweight 'Fighting Order', but on the trek to Sussex Mountain they carried their rifle, a minimum of seven full magazines, four grenades, two full water bottles, their entrenching tool, rations, webbing, and a Bergen containing washing kit, spare boots, sleeping bag and arctic clothing. Everyone carried extras, such as rockets for the 66mm or 84mm rocket launchers, bombs for the platoon 2in mortar, two or more bandoliers of ammunition for the GPMG, a weapon sight for their rifle, spare radio batteries or shells for the M79 grenade launcher.

the inadequacy of their boots became apparent practically from the moment they stepped foot in the Falklands. Equipment was standard 1958 pattern issue, together with a variety of rucksacks, a windproof suit, water bottle, poncho roll and lightweight shovel, to mention but a few items of 'kit' they carried. Weapons included the self-loading rifle, or SLR, with Trilux sight attached, which together functioned as the standard firearm for British infantry and paratroopers in 1982. Other weapons included the general purpose machine-gun (GPMG) – a modified 7.62mm form of the popular Bren light machine-gun from the Second World War – a direct-fire weapon with a range of 1,800m (2,000yd), which provided sustained fire when the gunner had a line of sight to his target. They also employed the much heavier .50 calibre machine-gun, meant for supporting fire against trenches, bunkers, sangars and light vehicles.

The Blowpipe, a surface-to-air missile meant to defend ground troops against aircraft attacking at low altitude, could be carried and deployed by an individual soldier. Radio or optical tracking guided the missile, which, with its high explosive warhead, weighted 21kg (47lb) and measured 4ft 7in in length. It was remarkably effective against dug-in enemy positions, but added considerably to the burden already borne by soldiers who, in the case of those who marched to Goose Green from the landing site on East Falkland, did so without the benefit of helicopter transport. An individual infantryman might also carry a Milan – a wire-guided missile fired from the shoulder – intended for use against armour, but which was discovered in the course of the campaign to prove highly effective against bunkers and sangars. Its guidance system relied simply on keeping the target in the cross hairs as the missile hurtled forward to a maximum range of 2,000m (2,200yd). The Milan's hollow-charge high explosive warhead could penetrate most armour plating and, as with the Blowpipe, proved devastating against Argentine trenches at Goose Green and then, only a fortnight later, against the defensive positions encountered in the mountains west of Stanley.

British Paratrooper

Members of 2 Para wore a windproof DPM parachute smock based on a version developed during the Second World War, together with over-trousers, all in camouflage of light green, yellow, light red-brown and black. They also carried foul-weather clothing, which consisted of thin rainproofs of various varieties, but for 2 Para usually constituted of an olive green waterproof smock lined in white. They wore a parachute brevet on the right sleeve of their smocks above a blue 'DZ patch' and rank chevrons. The new fibre paratrooper's helmet replaced the old metal version and was often worn with scrim nets, though paras often just wore their maroon regimental beret with dulled cap badge. Footwear came in the form of either the standard-issue 'boots DMS' or 'boots, high, combat'. Webbing consisted of 1958-pattern Combat Equipment Fighting Order (CEFO), an olive-green nylon rucksack and NBC (nuclear, biological and chemical) equipment. He often wore padded black leather 'Northern Ireland' gloves, carried a lightweight shovel and a self-loading rifle, better known as an SLR, which could mount a Trilux SUIT sight, which, however, the paras usually detached for close-quarter fighting or discarded altogether as useless under the Falklands' damp conditions.

Corporal (Cpl) John Geddes of C Company described the Paras' *raison d'être*:

Fire and move! Fire and move! That's the mantra of the infantryman and when's all said and done, motivated and well trained as they are, paras are infantrymen. They're just specialist infantry who can be dropped in on a battle from the air. The idea is to close with the enemy and not to sit in some shell scrape exchanging fire with him like insults. The idea is to get up close and personal and then kill the bastard.

British paratrooper in full kit.

Sgt Chris Howard, from the anti-tank platoon, 3 Para.

The standard 81mm mortar provided further support to the paras, firing at a rate of fifteen rounds per minute and sending ordnance with considerable accuracy to distances of between 4,500m and 5,600m, depending on the strength of the charge employed. Rounds weighed almost 4kg (10lb). The mortar itself weighed nearly 36kg (80lb) and required a three-man team to operate it as part of the specialist mortar platoon of the battalion's support company. Mortars could fire high explosive bombs, smoke or illuminating bombs. Crews were not supposed to strike targets closer than 200–300m from friendly forces, though in action they sometimes neglected this rule. The mortar's principal function was to act as mobile artillery, firing at very high angles and thus taking advantage of cover from walls, steep hills and gullies. The mortar also has a high rate of fire. At a normal rate of eight rounds a minute, the two mortars available to 2 Para would require eighty rounds to sustain fire for five minutes – and yet only about 500 bombs lay at the first baseplate position at the start of the action. The shortage of this vitally important support weapon would persuade the commanding officer to place his precious mortars in reserve, putting his faith in the more powerful fire support that the artillery and HMS *Arrow* could provide.

The paras tended to attack with two platoons 'up' – that is, forward – and one in reserve. In destroying trenches, they tended to crawl forward or make short bursts when under fire before employing whatever heavy weapons they had at their disposal, including 66mm rockets, as well as grenades. Trench-clearing in particular involved machine-guns and grenades, either white phosphorus (WP) or L2s – the standard high explosive. To illuminate a trench in the dark, infantry could fire a flare or call for mortar-fired illumination rounds. Often they could identify their enemy's position by identifying the source of the colourful lines of tracer fire, which lit up the night sky.

Communication in action posed all manner of problems, as individual soldiers did not have radio contact with their section or platoon commanders. Even for those in possession of the new Clansman radio, a reliable instrument, noise produced under fire could render communication difficult and sometimes impossible. During a mortar barrage on D Company, for instance, Second Lieutenant (2nd Lt) Chris Waddington found that command and control became a shambles when his men could not hear him shouting – and nor could he hear the sound of his own voice. The source of the cacophony of battle lay with bursting artillery shells, which upon impact with the soft peat produced a muffled crash; belt-fed machine-guns rattled off in a constant staccato; grenades exploded with a recognisable thump; and of course, rifle fire produced incessant popping. All forms of ordnance were easily distinguishable from one another, particularly for troops with long experience of exercises on Salisbury Plain or elsewhere, and even young soldiers could differentiate between distant and close rifle fire. Lieutenant (Lt) Peter Kennedy, C Company, noted how 'Enemy small arms fire began to fly past us, but buzzed like angry bees rather than the expected crack because they were reaching the limit of their range'. (Adkin, *Goose Green*, p. 206)

Members of 3 Para's anti-tank platoon, with machine-guns, move off Mount Longdon. Amongst other support weapons, an anti-tank platoon carried the Milan, a wire-guided missile fired from the shoulder for use against tanks. Troops soon discovered, however, that the Milan performed superbly against bunkers, trenches and houses.

Artillery supporting 2 Para at Goose Green came in the form of the 105mm light gun, which entered service shortly before the Falklands War, replacing the 105mm pack howitzer. It had a range of 14,500m, which, from the gunners' firing position at Camilla Creek House, meant that the artillery could cover the whole area of the isthmus without advancing the gun line. Six guns comprised a full battery, with a single weapon manned by a crew of six who provided an average rate of fire of three rounds per minute. On this basis, a battery was capable of bringing down fire on a target area at a rate of eighteen shells per minute. At Goose Green only three guns, or half a battery, were present. Rates of fire can vary, but with an expectation of 360 shells an hour over several hours, the rate of expenditure ought to have been high, were it not for the shortage of transport – especially helicopters capable of operating at night. Only a dozen Sea Kings were available to move the guns and their crews to the firing position at Camilla Creek House, in support of an operation meant to be fought almost entirely in

Helicopter on shipboard landing pad. Before the Atlantic Conveyor *went down the British had eleven Sea King and five Wessex helicopters as medium-lift aircraft. These could only operate during the day, since only four crews had training and a complement of night-vision goggles. With Stanley separated from San Carlos by 100km of inhospitable ground and with weather conditions deteriorating daily, helicopters became all the more vital for conveying troops and supplies forward.*

darkness. Specifically, three helicopters were required for the three guns, and a fourth for the twenty-eight personnel, leaving eight to ferry ammunition. Each helicopter could only move one box at a time, underslung in a net, with each box containing forty-eight shells. This only represented 384 shells, which, at an average rate of fire, would be exhausted in an hour.

The officer in command of the guns decided to send forward only high explosive (HE) shells on the basis that the targets almost certain to be encountered would include infantry defending trenches, vehicles and guns. HE rounds fired by the artillery could explode as airburst or point detonating (PD), with the former exploding 30ft above the ground and sending a shower of shrapnel over a wide area; the latter detonating once the shell made impact with the ground. At Goose Green, airburst shells suited the defender, since 2 Para attacked over exposed ground (bare terrain), whereas the British opted for PD rounds, since these were more effective against dug-in troops making use of trenches and bunkers. The British required no armour-piercing ammunition, since intelligence revealed that the Argentines possessed no tanks in the area. As the frigate HMS *Arrow*, lying offshore to the west of the isthmus, could fire star-shells from her powerful 4.5in main gun to partially illuminate the night sky, the artillery was not supplied with illumination rounds – which, in the event, proved short-sighted. Moreover, since 2 Para's mortars could provide smoke cover once dawn arrived, the British did not supply the guns with smoke rounds.

Responsibility for choosing targets for the guns rested with the gun position officer (GPO) at the gun line. To carry out this function he needed to know the location of the target, its type, the timing of fire, the type of ammunition required and the length of the barrage. All of this was provided by the forward observing officer (FOO) who positioned himself with the infantry, preferably so that he possessed line of sight to the target and could, consequently, observe the fall of the shells, thereby enabling him to order adjustments to targeting if necessary. Thus, the effectiveness of fire support depended heavily on the competence of FOOs. The battery commander stood forward with the infantry, as he had to be in place to advise the infantry commander on the role of artillery support. He collaborated on questions concerning fire support planning and moved about with the infantry commander in Tac 1, the battalion's headquarters, consisting of the CO and his staff. In action, the battery commander controlled the FOOs, determined the priority of targets, monitored ammunition expenditure and decided when and if the guns ought to bear on a different target as circumstances required. He seldom interfered with the actual firing of the guns, which took their direction from the FOOs via radio.

Lieutenant Colonel 'H' Jones VC, OBE, Commanding Officer of 2 Para

Born on 14 May 1940, the 42-year-old son of a wealthy West Country landowning family was better known as 'H' owing to his dislike of 'Herbert'. He attended Eton College before joining the Devon and Dorset Regiment in 1960, serving later in Northern Ireland and transferring to the Parachute Regiment in December 1979 as its commanding officer. Jones possessed a fiery temper, exuded boundless energy and believed strongly in the notion that officers lead from the front. Upon hearing news of the invasion while on a skiing holiday in the French Alps, Jones raced home and demanded that 2 Para form part of the Task Force, which already contained 3 Para. Mortally wounded on Darwin Hill at about 0930 hrs, 28 May, Jones received a posthumous Victoria Cross for, according to his citation, not only his own exemplary conduct, but for the impact of his unit on the campaign as a whole: 'The achievements of 2nd Battalion The Parachute Regiment at Darwin and Goose Green set the tone for the subsequent land victory on the Falklands. They achieved such a moral superiority over the enemy in this first battle that, despite the advantages of numbers and selection of battle-ground, they never thereafter doubted either the superior fighting qualities of the British troops, or their own inevitable defeat. This was an action of the utmost gallantry by a commanding officer whose dashing leadership and courage throughout the battle were an inspiration to all about him.'

His conduct and commendation have remained the object of controversy ever since. In his memoirs, Private (Pte) Tony Banks, D Company, expressed a commonly held opinion: 'My view is that Jones should never have been in that position [acting in the role of a section leader] in the first place. He was in the Falklands to lead the whole of 2 Para, not a small assault force. He was gung-ho and brave but irresponsible.' (Banks, *Storming the Falklands*, p. 125)

Lieutenant Colonel 'H' Jones VC, OBE.

THE DAYS BEFORE BATTLE:
OPPOSING PLANS AND DISPOSITIONS

The Argentine Plan of Defence

The British reacted rapidly to news of the Argentine invasion: on 5 April dispatching to the South Atlantic the carriers *Hermes* and *Invincible*, followed four days later by the *Canberra* carrying three Royal Marine commandos (40, 42 and 45, each the equivalent of a battalion in the army) and Third Battalion The Parachute Regiment (3 Para). This response was entirely unexpected by Galtieri's government, which now sought to reinforce its garrison, for as it stood, it did not comprise a force whose composition suited the role of repelling an expeditionary force tasked with recapturing the Falklands. Reinforcements dispatched from the mainland came in the form of 9 Brigade under Brigadier General (Brig. Gen.) Oscar Jofre, whose men arrived by air between 11 and 16 April and deployed around Stanley, with Jofre appointed land forces commander under the islands' overall commander and governor, Brig. Gen. Mario Menendez.

When senior Argentine commanders met in Buenos Aires on 22 April to devise their strategy of defence, holding Stanley stood at the forefront of their plan; well aware that its fall would mark the end of Argentine control – in Clausewitzian terms, the capital represented their opponent's 'centre of gravity'. The high command deemed the retention of West Falkland important, but not essential, for it contained only small, isolated settlements at Port Howard and Fox Bay. Even the area immediately across Falkland Sound – the western end of East Falkland, which included San Carlos and Darwin-Goose Green – strategists did not assess as critically important to hold. Sixty-five kilometres (40 miles) separated these positions from the outer ring of rocky eminences dotting the otherwise flat, bleak and boggy landscape immediately west of Stanley, and thus they calculated that their primary means of defence must hinge on holding the series of elevated points between Mount Kent and Wireless Ridge, the latter of which lay on the very fringe of the capital. In fact, Argentine commanders possessed but few alternatives to such a strategy, for by dint of their position as the defender, their troops did not enjoy the benefits of holding the initiative. Their approaching opponents on the other hand, while labouring under major disadvantages of their own – an extended logistics tail, warships and supply vessels vulnerable to air and naval attack, to name but a few – could profit from their ability to determine the point of attack, until that moment exercising the element of surprise.

The coastline extended for hundreds of miles and while Galtieri and most of his staff reckoned the British would effect a landing somewhere near Stanley, this deduction could only remain speculative until the Task Force actually made its appearance. Defending every beach and cove naturally presented a physical impossibility – and even after the landings took place, the British could, the Argentines reckoned with a reasonable degree of logic, deploy their forces rapidly by helicopter, subject to the degree to which they could successfully contest command of the air. In short, the defenders concentrated their forces in and around Stanley, on the basis that a landing elsewhere obliged the attacker to cover a great deal of ground before reaching their ultimate objective. Complicating matters still further for Menendez and his far-flung forces, the British might

THE SETTLEMENTS

Goose Green and its smaller, neighbouring settlement of Darwin sit on a narrow isthmus which separates Lafonia from the rest of East Falkland. This land bridge measures only 10km (6 miles) long and 2km (1.2 miles) wide. It is treeless, constantly swept by wind and consists of low ridges and open grassland rendered permanently soggy by constant precipitation and a high water table. In 1982, fewer than 150 people inhabited the two settlements combined, which constituted part of 'the Camp', the name given by the islanders to describe the largely unpopulated area – home to large numbers of grazing sheep – extending beyond the limits of Stanley.

open their offensive by launching a diversionary landing, thus drawing off the attention of the defenders before executing the main attack elsewhere. The Argentines considered the possibility of British landings at more than half a dozen locations across East Falkland – including the actual site, San Carlos – but its situation 90km (56 miles) from Stanley ruled it out from further consideration. In the end – and well before the arrival of the Task Force in hostile waters – the Argentines concentrated around the capital four infantry regiments, minus C Company 25th Regiment, which they deployed at Goose Green, and a further regiment on West Falkland.

Soon thereafter, while the Task Force continued its progress to the South Atlantic, the Argentines deployed another brigade to the islands, consisting of the 4th, 5th and 12th Regiments under Brig. Gen. Omar Parada. It did not enjoy a high standard of efficiency or experience and hailed from near the Uruguay border in the sub-tropical north – and thus was poorly acclimatised to the chilly conditions characteristic of the South Atlantic at that season, unlike brigades based in the far south of Argentina. Worse still, the high command dispatched these troops so hastily to the Falklands that many of the brigade's reservists did not reach the point of departure and thus it contained many recent recruits. Argentina might have sent a better-trained brigade, but they had held back the best personnel to monitor the border with Chile, with whom Buenos Aires harboured a long-term dispute over islands in Tierra del Fuego, and whom it was feared might take advantage of Argentina's temporary weakness and launch an attack.

With the last Argentine reinforcements reaching the islands in late April, Menendez, the land forces commander, now boasted a force of 13,000 troops, including about 6,000 infantry. Parada, Commander of 3 Brigade, controlled West Falkland where the 5th Regiment and 8th Regiment held Port Howard and Fox Bay, respectively. His command also included the tiny settlements of Darwin and Goose Green, situated on an isthmus that sits astride the southern land route from Stanley to San Carlos, via Fitzroy; the northern route is located north of the chain of mountains in the centre of East Falkland, which requires movement via Teal Inlet. The two settlements – they are not large enough to warrant

Disembarkation rehearsal for 2 Para aboard Norland. *Paras were used to deploying on operations via C-130 Hercules transport aircraft, not landing craft, and thus required at least rudimentary practice at what their amphibiously trained Royal Marines colleagues found second-nature. (Dr Stephen Hughes)*

Overall strength

In the Falklands as a whole, the Argentines enjoyed a clear numerical superiority – 13,000 men all told – as compared to about 8,000 ground personnel comprising the Task Force opposing them. The Argentines deployed forty-two 105mm pack howitzers and four 155mm guns, for forty-six pieces of artillery in total, as compared with thirty-six British guns of the Royal Artillery. But if the Argentines could bring more men and firepower to bear, the British more than compensated with troops of superior training, morale and motivation. In terms of weaponry, no appreciable difference stood between a British and Argentine soldier; but in terms of aggression and a 'will to win', the former possessed a clear advantage.

description as towns – together held 114 people. They existed solely for the purposes of supporting local sheep farming and consisted of little more than a few dozen structures: a store, a community centre, the manager's house, a school, shearing sheds and barns, and houses. This represented the only significant concentration of civil population in the west of the island and, together with the airstrip at Goose Green, necessitated that the Argentines provide a permanent garrison there. This included the 12th Regiment under Lt Col Italo Piaggi, who arrived on 24–25 April, replacing in command Lt Estoban, whose company took the place of B Company 12th Regiment, which had remained at Stanley as a strategic reserve. Piaggi also had a platoon detached from C Company 8th Regiment, whose parent unit remained at Fox Bay.

Piaggi spent weeks laying mines in the centre of the isthmus north of Darwin: behind the beaches on the western side; to the east, placed north of the school bridge; and just north of the airstrip and Goose Green settlement itself. Others were laid on Goose Green peninsula and further south. He was short of support weapons and HQ in Stanley had declined to send him any artillery, apart from his anti-aircraft guns. In all, this body of troops was known as Task Force Mercedes, named after the town where the 12th Regiment was based, and included twelve Pucara aircraft, four anti-aircraft guns and associated air force personnel. Piaggi's men were not only inexperienced but also lacked heavy equipment and support weapons, most of which were left behind in Argentina during the rush to dispatch troops to the islands. This materiel was meant to come by ship but never arrived, thus denying 12th Regiment all of its vehicles apart from three Land Rovers, commandeered from their local owners and allocated one each to A and C Companies and the Reconnaissance (Recce) Platoon. What little support weapons Piaggi had consisted of two 81mm and one 120mm mortars, although he ought to have had ten of the former and four of the latter. He was meant to have thirteen recoilless rifles but had only one. Of the normal complement of twenty-five light machine-guns he possessed fewer than half that number. He had no artillery apart from the anti-aircraft guns, which could indeed fire on ground targets, though their crews were not trained for this role. Piaggi's command thus suffered from numerous problems: poor training, a force lacking cohesion and homogeneity, indifferent morale, poor mobility and poor communications. Even though Parada believed an attack unlikely, since Stanley was assumed to be the most likely target, he nonetheless ordered Piaggi to undertake the necessary defensive measures at Darwin-Goose Green.

Piaggi's deployment reflected his inability to predict the direction and manner of attack, should the British decide to make a thrust in the Darwin-Goose Green area. His orders bade him to defend both settlements, as well as the airstrip. The air force personnel and guns were responsible for air defence, but Piaggi was left to defend against either a landward approach from the north, amphibious landings somewhere along the isthmus, or helicopter insertion, probably with a view to seizing the airstrip. Still, he understood that he could not hope to man the entire coastline with his three companies in case of seaborne attack, and thus satisfied himself with laying mines along part of the 10–12km (6–7.5 miles) of coastline

GOOSE GREEN IN ARGENTINE STRATEGY

Commanders on the Falklands assigned no particular value
to the Darwin-Goose Green area with respect to the overall
strategy of defending Stanley. The area stood a great
distance from the capital and even if the British captured
it – and there was no reason to believe they would – its loss
would have no effect on the defensive plan to hold Stanley.
The only reason it held a garrison was because of its airstrip,
which, apart from those on Pebble Island and at Stanley,
could provide facilities for Pucara aircraft.

and deploying his infantry principally near Goose Green. Manresa's
A Company 25th Regiment was positioned about 3km (1.8 miles)
north of Goose Green, occupying high ground west of Darwin, while
C Company 12th Regiment under Fernandez was deployed about
1.5km (0.9 miles) south-west of Goose Green on a low hill. This
did not entirely solve the dilemma of monitoring the beaches, but
from these positions the two companies could both observe the
coastline to east and west, and prevent an enemy moving along it
from north and south. This left Aliaga's C Company 8th Regiment,
which occupied ground near Salinas Beach to the west of Goose
Green, and Estoban's C Company 25th Regiment, which remained
in reserve at the settlement.

Even before the Task Force reached South Atlantic waters the
British opened hostilities when, before dawn on the morning of
1 May, an RAF Vulcan bomber struck Stanley airfield. In response,
Pucaras at Goose Green went aloft in search of a possible heliborne
landing by British troops, despite the fact that, unbeknownst to
the Argentines, the landings would not take place for another
three weeks. Two Pucaras, seeking to take off around 0725 hrs,
found themselves under attack by three British Harriers sent from
HMS *Hermes*.The Harrriers dropped cluster bombs on the airstrip,
destroying one Pucara and seriously damaging two others, leaving
five dead and fourteen wounded. Three Pucaras, already airborne

PIAGGI'S DECISIONS

By moving a platoon from 8th Regiment north to man the trenches near Boca House prior to B Company's reaching that objective, Piaggi thereby positioned a unit with a clear field of fire extending as far as 1,000m beyond the gorse line. Accordingly, although Crosland's men had made good progress against light resistance in the pre-dawn hours, Piaggi's decision proved a sound one, for this redeployment would hold up B Company for four hours, making a mockery of 2 Para's timetable.

and attempting to land an hour later, were redirected to Pebble Island, just north of West Falkland, owing to the closure of Goose Green's airstrip. A further four Pucaras were dispatched to Pebble Island in the forthcoming days until, on 14–15 May, D Squadron SAS raided the airstrip there and destroyed all eleven aircraft on the ground. On the same day, four more Pucaras arrived at Goose Green, but the catastrophe at Pebble Island persuaded the Argentines to remove them to the safety of Stanley lest they suffer the same fate. This left only three damaged aircraft at Goose Green, kept behind to serve as decoys. As such, the garrison comprised many air force personnel and several anti-aircraft guns, but no serviceable aircraft. Three more Harriers attacked the airfield on 14 May, but this time the anti-aircraft crews were ready and managed to shoot down one of them. As a result of the obvious danger of further British air attacks, the Argentines shifted some of their defensive positions closer to the houses of Goose Green settlement, together with helicopters, on the assumption that the British would not attack such structures. At the same time, they decided to concentrate all 114 residents of Darwin and Goose Green into the latter's community hall, on whose roof they painted a red cross. The garrison proceeded to occupy the residents' houses, which the troops plundered and rendered filthy with excrement deposited on floors and in baths.

Neither Piaggi at Goose Green nor his superiors at Stanley had any notion of where the British intended to land. Indeed, they assumed that air raids against Goose Green might continue, perhaps even an SAS raid undertaken – but the place did not seem a natural target of attack. Still, Piaggi kept his men busy constructing bunkers, digging trenches, laying mines and sending out patrols. His troop dispositions, however, remained unchanged, apart from his response on 15 May to growing anxiety over the presence of British ships in Falkland Sound. As a result of these anxieties, Piaggi received orders to establish an observation point at Port San Carlos, which he did with one platoon, two anti-aircraft guns and two mortars, plus a detachment at Fanning Head, 10km (6 miles) away. Quite unbeknownst to Piaggi, 3 Commando Brigade had already designated San Carlos as its landing site in five days' time.

British Plans and Landings

While the operational name for the expedition as a whole was known as 'Corporate', for the actual landings themselves the British applied the code name 'Sutton'. A great deal of thought and planning went into choosing the landing site. Brig. Julian Thompson RM and Commodore Michael Clapp RN, who commanded the amphibious task group with responsibility for landing the troops and supplies, wished ideally to land unobserved. If this proved impossible, they hoped at least to arrive unopposed, as landing craft crowded with troops are extremely vulnerable to artillery, mortar- and machine-gun fire, not to mention aircraft. British strategic planners sought to meet several criteria: a landing site composed of beaches whose sand consisted of sufficient firmness to admit landing craft and offloaded vehicles; a site that permitted an approach by night; a site around which a perimeter defence could be established to successfully oppose a counter-attack; and a site situated within a reasonable distance of Stanley, the final objective.

2 Para undergoes physical training on the deck of Norland. *The Parachute Regiment prides itself on the extremely high standard of fitness demanded of its men, who alternated by company in running round the ship's decks as part of the regular, rigorous exercise regime carried out during the seven-week journey to the South Atlantic.*

Thompson issued orders for Operation *Sutton* from HMS *Fearless* on 13 May, and would assume command of all land forces approximately a week after the first landings. In the meantime, with 3 Commando Brigade nearing the islands and 5 Infantry Brigade on its way south, Thompson led 3 Commando Brigade only. He was to secure a bridgehead on East Falkland, establish a defensive perimeter around it so that reinforcements could be brought in, gather intelligence on the strength and intentions of the enemy, and 'establish moral and physical domination over the enemy, and further the ultimate objective of repossession'. These aims, the likelihood of whose attainment increased with 5 Infantry Brigade's arrival about a week later, would set the stage for the offensive across East Falkland, which was to follow in the wake of the landings.

Planners began the process of selecting landing sites by carefully studying a detailed map of the Falklands and took advice from Maj. Ewan Southby-Tailyour, whose yachting around the islands during prior service with the Royal Marines garrison had furnished him with an intimate knowledge of the entire coastline and tides. Nineteen beaches were considered, until the planners reduced these down to three: Cow Bay/Volunteer Bay, Berkeley Sound and San Carlos, ultimately selecting the last of these as it met all their criteria. Although it happened to be much further from Stanley, this factor alone did not impose insurmountable obstacles. Paradoxically, in fact, the site's considerable distance to the capital lent a degree of advantage, insofar as it introduced the element of surprise, since the Argentines were unlikely to suspect it as a landing site. Indeed, early intelligence gathered by the Special Boat Service (SBS) indicated no enemy presence in the area, with the nearest Argentines 30km (18.6 miles) away at Goose Green, where Thompson's intelligence officer reckoned the garrison strength at 300–500 men, possibly with some artillery, anti-aircraft guns and assorted air force personnel. There always remained the possibility of heliborne reinforcement from garrisons further east but, for the moment, circumstances for an amphibious operation appeared very favourable.

The landings were to take place at night owing to the absence of British air superiority. 2 Para would be the first ashore. All units would then establish defensive positions in order to resist an expected Argentine response by land and air once daylight appeared. Artillery and Rapier anti-aircraft batteries would be landed at first light by helicopter. No detailed explanation of the landings need concern us here, apart from 2 Para's. While other units would establish a defensive position near their own landing sites and form a base from which to launch an advance on Stanley, 2 Para was to advance to Sussex Mountain, immediately to the south, to dig in, erect barbed wire and lay mines. This was vital ground, since it would help secure the beachhead and provide a commanding view of the whole area for miles around.

At about 0430 hrs on Friday 21 May, the SAS launched a diversionary attack just north of Darwin with the mistaken belief that the Argentines possessed a strategic reserve in the area, which could pose a threat to Operation *Sutton*. Approximately forty SAS troopers opened fire on Manresa's A Company, but they did not seek to engage it for any period, much less attempt to dislodge it. Piaggi reported the raid, but was, as yet, unaware of the landings further north. 'H-Hour' – the time when the landing craft were meant to disgorge their troops on the beaches – was set for 0230 hrs on Friday 21 May. This would give 2 Para four hours of darkness with which to reach and ascend Sussex Mountain, dig in and ready themselves for any attempt by the garrison at Darwin-Goose Green to oppose the establishment of a beachhead by the other four battalions. In fact, a small force of Argentines was positioned at Fanning Head and sighted the ships offshore, before the SBS drove them off. Landing craft, involving the whole of 3 Commando Brigade, duly put ashore five elite battalions – 2 and 3 Para; 40, 42 and 45 Commando Royal Marines – from 0430 hrs, with three more battalions scheduled to arrive nine days later.

2 Para was the first unit to disembark, but the landing craft carrying its individual companies lowered their doors in more than 1ft of water, so the troops became wet the moment they stepped out on to what they expected to be more or less dry sand.

British landing craft. 2 and 3 Para, plus 40, 42 and 45 Commando Royal Marines all came ashore by this means before dawn on 21 May. Entering San Carlos Water, 2 Para and 40 Commando landed at San Carlos Settlement, 3 Para and 42 Commando at Port San Carlos, and 45 Commando just north of Ajax Bay.

From there, the priority was to reach the top of Sussex Mountain before the Argentines at Darwin-Goose Green decided to deny it to them. But 2 Para was behind schedule in their endeavour to arrive at their objective by dawn. The landings took place late, with 2 Para leaving their craft at approximately 0430 hrs instead of 0230 hrs. Sunrise then came at 0630 hrs – too late to allow the paras to reach the top of Sussex Mountain in darkness. A good deal of time was also wasted on the beach trying to organise the men into their correct sub-units and establish a proper order of march. The distance also confounded the timetable, for the 8km (5 mile) route was uphill and the battalion heavily encumbered by overloaded Bergens. Nothing but slow movement could be expected, especially for those carrying Milans, machine-guns, mortars or Blowpipes. Even before the troops left the beaches, the shortage of helicopters required them to carry artillery shells, Rapiers, bulk ammunition and stores. Jones' men, like their comrades in 3 Para and the three RM commandos, had to carry enough food and ammunition for two days of fighting, plus two 81mm mortar bombs and a host of other items, weighing in all at least 50kg (110lb). Moreover, 2 Para, like practically everyone else, were partly wet with no possibility of drying out – a serious threat to the troops' health amidst prevailing winter conditions.

At dawn on the 21st, the paras reached the top of the 240m (800ft) Sussex Mountain, which stood unoccupied – though Argentine aircraft spotted the troops' presence. Meanwhile, at Goose Green, Vice-Commodore Pedroza ordered four of his six Pucaras to fly to San Carlos Water and return with a report. One was hit and downed by a Stinger fired by the SAS, its pilot ejecting; another failed to take off owing to HMS *Ardent* shelling the airfield. Sea Harriers attacked the other two over San Carlos; one escaped and the other was shot down, the ejecting pilot reaching the ground safely by parachute before walking back to Goose Green.

As discussed, Thompson planned to shift his troops east from around San Carlos in an offensive against Stanley. Time was of the essence, since the onset of winter meant he must capture

TRACER AMMUNITION

By their different colours, the firework-like brightness of tracer ammunition trails appearing in the night sky readily identified the nationality of the troops firing it: green or white for the Argentines and red for the British. The British also fired parachute illuminating and other flares to aid their visibility, which before sunrise around 0600 hrs cast light only a few metres.

his objective and secure repossession of the islands in the next three weeks. Otherwise, the campaign would grind to a halt as temperatures dropped, snow fell, winds increased – thus endangering helicopters – and the seas became too choppy for Harriers to take off and land, and for the ships of the Royal Fleet Auxiliary, civilian supply vessels and warships of the Royal Navy to operate safely. While he prepared plans to shift the bulk of his forces east, Thompson met with Jones early on the morning of 22 May and told him he wanted 2 Para to conduct a raid on Goose Green, consistent with orders from Northwood 'to establish moral and physical domination over the enemy'. This pleased Jones immensely, as his unit would clinch the first opportunity to come to serious grips with the Argentines.

The idea for the raid arose out of pressure exerted from London for a rapid advance once the troops landed. The government wanted swift action and the chiefs-of-staff were happy to oblige. Thompson planned to move his five battalions, plus 5 Infantry Brigade, to Mount Kent as soon as possible for a push against the ring of mountain defences west of Stanley. At the same time, Jones spent 23 and 24 May planning the conduct of his raid. The intelligence in his possession, supplied by the SAS, suggested the presence of only a single company of infantry (approx 100 men), though Capt. Alan Coulson, Jones' intelligence officer, thought this suspiciously low. Be that as it may, when Jones learned he had no helicopters at his disposal for moving his troops, he scrapped his initial plan to move his men by air. His proposal for a seaborne approach Thompson also turned down, since it involved various perils, including moving by night up Brenton Loch and landing at Salinas Beach opposite Goose Green. Navigation among the rocks would require radar, the detection of which would alert the Argentines and scupper the mission.

Without sufficient helicopters and in the absence of air superiority, Jones therefore concluded that the advance must be made on foot. Thompson approved his altered plan on the 24th and Jones duly briefed his company commanders. Paras from D Company began moving off Sussex Mountain as night fell on 25 May, with a total distance of 15km (9.3 miles) to be covered to Camilla Creek House, the battalion's start line for the raid. But as the paras reached about halfway to Camilla Creek House, Jones radioed with news that the raid had been cancelled; the weather was deteriorating and even the helicopter pilots equipped with night vision could not fly, thus rendering it impossible to move forward the artillery meant for 2 Para's support. Without guns, the raid was likely to fail. Jones, well known for his short fuse and fiery temper, was furious and made his thoughts abundantly clear to all around him.

Preparations for Battle

Fortunately for Jones, Whitehall demanded immediate action from Thompson, who was himself keen to advance but feeling constrained by the lack of helicopter lift to move his forces to Mount Kent, the staging area for the final advance on Stanley. Pressure arose from many sources owing to the mounting losses of ships in the week of the landings, and the fact that, with the beachhead established and not itself under attack, nothing appeared to prevent 3 Commando Brigade from moving out and taking the fight to the Argentines. Parliament, press and public were also keen for some sort of (successful) engagement and an early termination of the war. On the diplomatic front, too, Thatcher's government grew concerned that the mounting international call for a ceasefire would leave British forces in a perilous situation, paralysed by inertia at San Carlos with the worst of winter imminent. Admiral Sir John Fieldhouse, at Northwood, as well as the other chiefs-of-staff also wanted Thompson to assume the initiative, break out of the beachhead and engage the Argentines. Politicians, the military and the public all expected the Task Force to deliver a short, sharp, decisive blow, resulting in the repossession of the Falklands and South Georgia. Not surprisingly, then, despite its relative insignificance in military terms, Goose Green became the focus of Thompson's attentions.

Naturally, like any commander 'on the ground', Thompson understood the logistical constraints better than anyone and perfectly appreciated that, notwithstanding his keenness to advance, he required the heavy-lift capacity of helicopter transport so fundamentally important to an operation of this kind. Eleven of these vital machines were aboard a 15,000-ton requisitioned civilian container ship called the *Atlantic Conveyor*, due to arrive late on the 25th. Unfortunately, on the same day, an Exocet missile struck her, causing a massive fire that destroyed three Chinooks, six Wessex and one Lynx, as well as tons of supplies. One Chinook, auspiciously airborne at the time of the attack, landed safely on another vessel – but the loss of ten helicopters represented a serious blow both to Thompson's mobility and to his system of supply. In short, his plan to convey infantry and marines to Mount Kent by helicopter had to be drastically altered, severely limiting his options for an immediate blow to be struck against the Argentines – including the bringing up of 5 Infantry Brigade, which was approaching East Falkland but still about five days away. Thompson could now recce Mount Kent but could not move his troops rapidly, as originally hoped.

Northwood would have none of it, and even as news of the loss of the *Atlantic Conveyor* became known at home, strategists intervened and resurrected the idea of an attack on Goose Green,

Chinook at night. Both sides suffered from acute shortages of these aircraft, especially the British, who lost ten helicopters when an Exocet missile fired from an Argentine fighter sank the container ship Atlantic Conveyor *on 25 May. 'We'll have to bloody well walk,' one of Thompson's staff concluded, referring to the necessity of marching some of the troops across East Falkland towards the final objective – Stanley.*

overriding Thompson's objections that he could furnish no artillery support for 2 Para. New instructions directed him to attack Goose Green without fire support, if necessary. For this task, the brigade commander retasked 2 Para on the 26th to prepare itself for a raid – much to Jones' exultation. The battalion moved out that night. The main thrust east also took shape: although Thompson could move 42 Commando by helicopter, early on the 27th he ordered 3 Para and 45 Commando to proceed on foot, leaving the deeply frustrated 40 Commando to provide security for the now expanded beachhead and the vital supply depot and medical facility at Ajax Bay. 2 Para, meanwhile, would also advance on foot, but only via the much shorter route to Camilla Creek House, from which Jones planned to launch not merely a raid, but a full-scale battalion attack.

The Argentines, meanwhile, could do little in response to the landings. Their forces on West Falkland possessed no transport and there were insufficient numbers of helicopters with which to convey troops from Stanley. To expect their infantry to move by foot was absolutely out of the question: traversing 80km (50 miles) with troops whose fitness bore no relation whatsoever to that of the paras and marines, while under possible British air attack, and with no means of shifting supplies forward over open ground, seemed to Menendez foolhardy in the extreme. When the junta proposed this very plan, Menendez refused, citing arguments whose wisdom his superiors felt grudgingly obliged to accept. Besides, the landings around San Carlos could still constitute a diversion to the main landings elsewhere, so denuding troops from the Stanley area appeared inadvisable. A counterstroke from Goose Green also seemed impractical, since the 12th Regiment constituted an under-strength regiment without artillery support or transport. The British, on the other hand, occupied high ground, in greater numbers, with naval gunfire and aircraft at their disposal. The best Menendez and Parada could do was reinforce Goose Green with two 105mm pack howitzers, only one of which reached Piaggi after an air attack grounded the vessel carrying them. These guns were, however, supplemented by two more flown in some days later. In short, Menendez, like Thompson, came under considerable pressure to take action: in the case of the former, now that the Argentine high command determined that San Carlos was not a diversion; in the case of the latter, owing to pressure to get on with the job. Ironically, therefore, almost precisely at the same moment as the Argentines accepted the impossibility of moving west on foot across East Falkland, Thompson was proposing to do precisely this – but obviously moving east instead of west – with elements of his own, albeit better trained, disciplined and motivated forces.

During this period, the Argentines launched a series of furious air attacks on the flotilla in Falkland Sound, later dubbed 'Bomb

Alley'. Between 21 and 25 May their air force flew approximately 180 sorties from the mainland, sustaining losses of nineteen aircraft but sinking the destroyer HMS *Coventry*, the frigates *Ardent* and *Antelope*, and the previously mentioned, all-important supply ship, *Atlantic Conveyor*. Several other ships were also severely damaged, including a destroyer, two frigates and two supply ships. The Argentines killed seventy-seven British – mostly naval – personnel, but by concentrating their attacks on warships rather than supply vessels they committed a critical strategic error, since without supplies Thompson could not have advanced across East Falkland – thus making the maritime logistic tail of the Task Force its 'centre of gravity'. The loss of the *Atlantic Conveyor* had already profoundly affected the brigadier's plans; and any further damage to logistics would doom the landing force to remain around its base at San Carlos – or withdraw altogether. On the other hand, the Argentines' problems were compounded by the fact that many of their bombs struck a host of vessels, yet failed to explode owing to mistimed fuses. Thus, with greater technical expertise and the acquisition of the right targets, the Argentines enjoyed a narrow but genuine window of opportunity to fatally compromise Operation *Corporate* within a week of *Sutton*.

In all, 2 Para spent six days on Sussex Mountain exposed to freezing wind, bereft of any natural cover – and with none to be found by digging in, for ubiquitous mist and precipitation kept the soil perpetually wet and the high water table permitted freezing water to fill trenches even before they reached a depth suitable to offer protection. The troops' boots failed to keep the damp out and trench foot resulted from permanently wet socks. These conditions, together with lack of warmth, poor rations and inadequate supplies of water took their toll on morale. Fortunately for Jones' men, the Argentines made air strikes against Sussex Mountain a low priority, as they concentrated their efforts against the ships off San Carlos; otherwise, 2 Para might have fared badly, especially since the Rapier air-defence system proved very inadequate to the task.

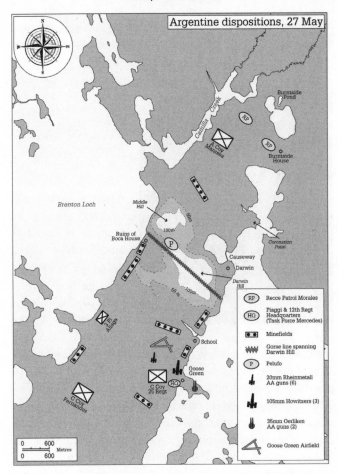

Argentine dispositions, 27 May

RP	Recce Patrol Morales
HQ	Piaggi & 12th Regt Headquarters (Task Force Mercedes)
■■■	Minefields
⋀⋀⋀⋀	Gorse line spanning Darwin Hill
P	Pelufo
	20mm Rheinmetall AA guns (6)
	105mm Howitzers (3)
	35mm Oerliken AA guns (2)
	Goose Green Airfield

At last, very late on the evening of 26 May, Jones ordered his battalion off the mountain for the four-to-five-hour march to Camilla Creek House, the designated assembly area, where the troops could rest before the attack went in and the CO and his staff could plan it. This proved another exhausting and slow march under exceedingly heavy loads, with several more paras falling out with ankle or other injuries sustained from the irregular surface of the ground. Ruts, rocks and the cursed 'babies' heads'

Paras with an Argentine prisoner. Jones specifically warned his men that he would not tolerate any abuse of their captives. Anyone caught doing so would be cast out of the regiment, irrespective of any subsequent legal action taken against the perpetrator.

– stalwart, thick tufts of grass – could all easily twist a knee or ankle, while fatigue led some men even to fall asleep during halts called to close the gaps in the snake-like column. D Company, the first to approach the house at 0300 hrs and unaware of any Argentine presence inside, called in an artillery strike, which proved inaccurate. In any event, they found the house and other buildings deserted. When 2 Para arrived at Camilla Creek House, Jones understood the risk of allowing everyone to cram themselves inside since the position made a marvellous target for artillery or an air strike. Still, with soldiers desperate for shelter and warmth, he permitted the 450 men (minus patrols and sentries) to occupy whatever space they could in the house, sheds and outbuildings, resulting in dozens of men sleeping across one another in a massive jumble, or alternatively squeezed into cupboards, spread across tables and stretched along shelves.

In the early hours of the 27th, two patrols moved off to await dawn. They were to observe the Argentine positions down the isthmus, allowing Jones and his staff to make an assessment of their strength and dispositions, so supplementing intelligence already supplied by the SAS, some of it based on observations made from a hide cleverly situated in a derelict vessel on the opposite side of Choiseul Sound. Jones was particularly anxious to learn the position of the 105mm guns so he could later call in an air strike, without having to employ the guns attached to his battle group for fear of revealing their positions. When first light appeared, the patrol observed a line of trenches and troops extending across the isthmus towards Burntside House to the east. Five trenches were spotted near the remains of Boca House to the west, plus a platoon position on slightly elevated ground near Camilla Creek. On the high ground west of Darwin one patrol counted sixteen trenches and a line of thick gorse stretching across the top of Darwin Hill. Neither patrol, which radioed back some of their observations, could locate any artillery. In any event, at about 0430 hrs Jones was told by Brigade HQ that poor weather had rendered flights impossible, so his plan to neutralise the guns from the air before the ground attack began came to naught.

Some hours later, however, Jones put in a renewed request for an air strike, as the weather was improving and he now possessed specific grid references and target descriptions provided by the patrols. Harriers duly arrived, but on their first pass could not identify the Argentine positions and so dropped their bombs during their second pass in hopes of hitting something – but without success. On their third pass, one Harrier was shot down. Still, a patrol captured some Argentines, including 12th Regiment's Recce Platoon commander, Lt Morales, plus a Land Rover – a great benefit in light of the fact that 2 Para's vehicles were still all aboard ship. The prisoners were duly interrogated, revealing further intelligence of the enemy's strength and dispositions.

Matters turned very much for the worse, however, when Battalion HQ tuned into the BBC World Service at 1000 hrs. They could not believe their ears when a journalist announced that 'a parachute battalion is poised and ready to assault Darwin

The battlefield of Goose Green, noteworthy for its almost complete lack of cover or 'dead ground'. (Dr Stephen Hughes)

and Goose Green' – an entirely accurate summation of Jones' intention. The colonel became apoplectic and the rest of the men at Camilla Creek House stood stunned at this unaccountable breach of security. There was no choice but to disperse the men from the buildings for their own protection in case the Argentines took the report at face value. Fortunately for 2 Para, they did not, for they quite naturally regarded the broadcast as nothing more than a childish attempt at disinformation; a deliberate ruse to distract their attention from some other, unknown point of attack. Jones, in any event, had to proceed with his plan notwithstanding.

Fortuitously for him, although his patrols could not penetrate down the isthmus, they were gathering quite useful and accurate intelligence. At 1130 hrs, one patrol was spotted and fired upon with machine-guns and automatic rifles, forcing its withdrawal behind a smoke screen, and about half an hour later the other patrol, still unseen, withdrew. Just before – with the air clearing and in response to Jones' renewed request for an air strike and the fact that he now possessed specific grid references and target descriptions provided by the patrols – two Harriers approached, moving south-east over the isthmus, and dropped cluster bombs which, however, failed to hit Burntside House. The other plane went down from anti-aircraft fire which blew off its tail and forced its pilot to eject.

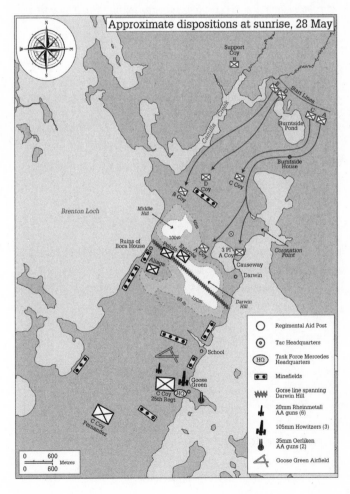

At about 1430 hrs, one of the patrols returned to Camilla Creek House and was debriefed by Jones who, now armed with some decent intelligence on Argentine positions, finalised his orders for the following day's assault and called together an 'Orders' or 'O' group at 1500 hrs to explain how the battalion was to execute its attack. The intelligence officer, Lt Coulson, was in the midst of his briefing when Jones, anxious to speed the process, interrupted him and explained his complex, six-phase, night/day, silent/noisy attack, which may be summarised as follows:

Phase One

Support Company to establish a firebase at the western end of Camilla Creek.

C Company to secure the Start Line at the junction of Camilla Creek and Ceritos Arroyo stream and then become Battalion reserve.

Phase Two: 0200 hrs

A Company to attack the right flank of 12th Infantry Regiment towards Darwin Hill.
B Company to attack the left flank around the derelict foundations of Boca House.

Phase Three: 0300 hrs

A Company to attack Coronation Point.
D Company to deal with a platoon position on high ground 1,000m north of Boca House.

Phase Four: 0400 hrs

B Company to attack Boca House.

Phase Five: 0500 hrs

> A Company to exploit to Darwin.
> C Company to push through B and D Companies to clear the airfield.

Phase Six: By 0600 hrs

> A Company to take Darwin.
> B Company to attack platoon from 25th Infantry Regiment at the schoolhouse.
> C Company to move into a blocking position south of Goose Green.
> D Company to liberate Goose Green.

Strict adherence to his plan would allow the rifle companies fourteen hours of darkness in which to clear the 6,000m to Goose Green: nine hours to prepare for action and to move to the battalion's start line; and the remaining five hours for the actual fighting against opponents well ensconced across largely open ground, by troops unaccustomed to night-fighting. Jones' timings were very short; the companies, platoons and sections possessed limited information on the Argentine dispositions in front of them; and everyone was tired, having acquired very little sleep since leaving Sussex Mountain where conditions were hardly conducive to comfort. Several company commanders did not feel they understood their instructions and some of this confusion was reflected down the chain of command, a process minutely examined by Spencer Fitz-Gibbon's post mortem of events in his extremely detailed, highly analytical but controversial study, *Not Mentioned in Dispatches: The History and Mythology of the Battle of Goose Green*. Yet, if unease about Jones' plan circulated amongst his subordinates, at least a few guns were now certain to make an appearance in the coming action, for that night, the 27th, Sea Kings from 846 Naval Air Squadron

Goose Green as seen from the gorse line. Reaching the settlement from here required an advance of between 1–2km (0.6–1.2 miles) of ground, depending on the direction of approach – much of it under heavy fire – and the capture first of the flagpole position and schoolhouse.

began lifting three guns of 8 Battery 29 Commando Regiment to Camilla Creek House. Here, it established a firing position well clear of the house to the north. By midnight, the gunners were ready to fire.

Piaggi, in the meantime, had not been idle. Once HQ in Stanley realised that the landings at San Carlos did not constitute a diversion they ordered Piaggi to cover the northern end of the isthmus as well as the south. As an attack from the north would have to come between Camilla Creek and Burntside House, defending this approach would, in theory, prevent penetration down the isthmus. Since this neck of land was narrow, this ought to have presented Piaggi with little difficulty. In fact, it was rather more complicated than this, for Parada instructed Piaggi to expand his defence of the north – yet at the same time he was not allowed to abandon other areas of defence in order to do so. This naturally thinned out his troops even more, for he had to continue to monitor the beaches, Goose Green, the airfield, the area south of Goose Green, and occupy the main defensive line west of Darwin and Darwin itself. To cover this whole area would require extending his troops out over 30km (19 miles), thus obliging him to violate the vital principle of concentration of force and denying his companies the ability to offer supporting fire to one another.

Parada's new instructions left Piaggi to place his three companies in the best possible disposition, which resulted in an unsatisfactory compromise, consisting of one company facing north from a position just west of Darwin, the main defensive line; another facing south from beyond Goose Green; and a third maintained as a reserve, to move once the direction of the attack became known. This troop dispersion, while it went some degree in covering a wide area, denied Piaggi's companies mutual support by separating those deployed in the north and south, respectively, by 4km (2.5 miles). True, he had laid mines to protect some of the beaches, the airfield and his main defensive line, but not all of

Looking across the water from the gorse line. The main Argentine defence line stretched across the isthmus from this point, with the ruins of Boca House on its western, and Darwin on its eastern, flank. Defenders manning the trenches in the position shown here held up both A and B Companies long enough to oblige 2 Para to fight ten of the fourteen hours of the battle in daylight – precisely the scenario that Jones sought to avoid.

these minefields benefitted from covering fire, a circumstance that left them vulnerable to penetration by engineers who could clear them quickly so long as they could operate without coming under fire in the process.

With so few troops at his disposal, Piaggi faced an impossible task in trying to provide an all-round defence. He commanded a mixed command of army, navy and air force components, with a maximum of 550 actual infantry. He lacked B Company 25th Regiment, a sub-unit detached earlier and now deployed north of Mount Kent; two of his platoons had been sent to Fanning Head and had not returned – one dispersed by naval gunfire and the other captured on the day of the British landings. Piaggi possessed only nine rifle platoons, consisting of three from A Company, three from B Company and two from C Company 25th Regiment, plus one from C Company 8th Regiment. In addition to these, he had a hybrid company under Lt Pelufo and a Recce Platoon – now lacking their commander, Lt Morales, who with a few men, as described earlier, had fallen captive to a patrol. Thus, in all, the Argentines at Goose Green comprised no more than eleven rifle platoons – a force that matched perfectly the number 2 Para would deploy for the battle. In overall numbers, 2 Para was outnumbered by two to one when accounting for all the Argentine infantry, engineers, various air force personnel including anti-aircraft gunners and ground crew, staff, and a handful of naval personnel. But in terms of infantry on the ground – that is to say, those best prepared to contest control of the two settlements – the opposing forces stood almost exactly equal in strength.

The virtual equality of opposing forces was reflected in their supporting weapons as well, for both sides deployed three 105mm guns. 2 Para looked forward to the firepower of HMS *Arrow's* 4.5in gun, as well, though the Argentines deployed anti-aircraft guns, which could lay fire down on the ground, again evening up the odds. Both sides lacked mortars and machine-guns. Most of 2 Para's were left behind by Support Company, while many of Piaggi's weapons were not shipped out with his infantry. Both

Looking down from the main Argentine defence position. Given the open nature of the ground, one is struck by the audacity – or foolhardiness, depending on one's perspective – required to attack it. Some frightened, raw Argentine recruits, lying prone or curled up in the foetal position, took refuge in the trenches under blankets or in sleeping bags, thus rendering themselves non-participants in the action. Most, however, emboldened by the protection afforded by their entrenchments, offered stiff resistance.

sides hoped for some air support: Piaggi needed Pucaras while Jones expected Harriers and helicopters.

On the 27th, on the eve of action – which Piaggi now anticipated in light of Morales' disappearance and observation of a hostile patrol – Piaggi received orders to move his defences north. Believing it vital to keep one of his companies in the south, and a reserve company around Goose Green itself, he shifted Manresa's A Company out of their trenches extending across the ridge west of Darwin, to a line running between the Low Pass and Burntside House. This required them to dig new trenches in a hurry.

There was no time to establish a minefield to their front and the move resulted in a widening of the already considerable gap existing between A and C Companies – now amounting to 7km (4.3 miles). It also meant weakening the hitherto strong position west of Darwin, for all Piaggi now had to fill the gap created by Manresa's company was Pelufo's mixed platoon – not an ideal deployment, since these comprised a mixed, composite bag of troops. Significantly, moreover, no one bothered to occupy Darwin Hill.

The scene was now set for the first ground action of the campaign – with the men of 2 Para barely having slept in thirty-six hours.

THE BATTLEFIELD:
WHAT ACTUALLY HAPPENED?

The Assault Begins

27 May	**2200 hrs**	Rifle Companies move off towards their respective start lines; Capt. Arnold, Naval Gunfire Officer (NGFO), begins calling down fire on pre-determined targets
28 May	**0145 hrs**	NGFO begins registering HMS *Arrow*'s fire on to A Company's first objective: Burntside House
	0200 hrs	Intended time for A Company (Farrar-Hockley) to advance on Burntside House; after firing a few rounds and a star shell, the main armament of HMS *Arrow* jams; 2 Para's support now confined to 3 x 105mm guns of 8 (Alma) Commando Battery, 3 x 81mm mortars, GPMGs and Milans
	0235 hrs	A Company begins advance, 35 minutes late, via bridge crossing over Ceritos Arroyo Stream, with Burntside House its first objective
	0250 hrs	British artillery opens fire on Burntside House as A Company approaches
	0252 hrs	A Company makes first contact with Argentines at Burntside House

28 May	0300 hrs	B Company (Crosland) leaves its start line and begins its advance down the west side of the isthmus towards its first objective, Boca House; D Company (Neame) remains in reserve
	0315 hrs	105mm shells from three guns of 8 Battery begin to fall on Burntside Hill
	0400 hrs	B Company reports successful taking of Burntside Hill; *Arrow*'s main armament resumes firing – some illuminating rounds and high explosive – onto Goose Green airfield
	0414 hrs	A Company in occupation of Burntside House
	0421 hrs	A Company resumes movement after reorganising in darkness
	0427 hrs	A Company reports no casualties and no enemy in contact
	0430 hrs	B Company crests Middle Hill. After an hour idle west of Burntside House, A Company resumes its advance by Jones' order
	0445 hrs	HMS *Arrow* leaves waters off Goose Green isthmus

Responsibility for ensuring that A Company reached its start line rested with Lt Colin Connor, the Recce Platoon commander. A Company was to advance on Burntside House at 0200 hrs from a line of fences running north–south, approximately 500m east of the house. Difficulty lay in finding the correct fence in the pitch black, marking out the position and sending guides to the battalion rendezvous (RV), which stood on a bridge over the Ceritos Arroyo stream. The guides would then lead A Company to the start line – a distance of about 2,000m across small streams and boggy ground. Connor managed the navigation correctly, but he was running behind schedule. Maj. Farrar-Hockley's A Company reached the start line and would begin its advance thirty-five minutes late. Support Company was next to move off, leaving Camilla Creek House at 1900 hrs on the 27th and establishing itself in its desired position

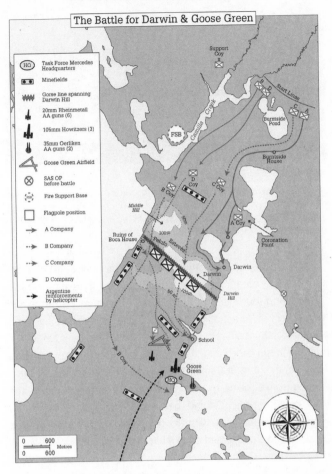

The Battle for Darwin & Goose Green

HQ	Task Force Mercedes Headquarters
	Minefields
	Gorse line spanning Darwin Hill
	20mm Rheinmetall AA guns (6)
	105mm Howitzers (3)
	35mm Oerliken AA guns (2)
	Goose Green Airfield
	SAS OP before battle
	Fire Support Base
	Flagpole position
	A Company
	B Company
	C Company
	D Company
	Argentine reinforcements by helicopter

overlooking Camilla Creek by 2200 hrs. There it waited until 0300 hrs on the 28th before it stood in a position to engage the Argentines. Finally, A Company left Camilla Creek House at 2220 hrs. All movement took place over sodden ground, which soaked the men's feet in icy water, the discomfort exacerbated by bitterly cold temperatures and rainfall beginning in the early hours of the morning. The night was completely black and no one could see the objectives.

A modern aerial view of the settlement at Goose Green, looking southwest towards Choiseul Sound. In theory the isthmus offered numerous opportunities for an attacker to strike from the sea, but rocks along the coast and mines laid just behind many of the beaches precluded this option. (Author)

Farrar-Hockley's A Company was first into the attack – in complete darkness, but not throughout, as the fighting was destined to last a staggering fourteen hours – realising afterwards his mistake in leaving behind the platoon 2in mortars. Still, his FOO had registered two targets: Burntside House and tents thought to be 500m to the right, near Burntside Pond. Accordingly, as A Company prepared to advance, the guns at Camilla Creek House began to fire, instantly shifting from a 'silent' to a 'noisy' attack. Since Capt. Watson, the FOO, could not see anything, he directed fire on the basis of the original grid references, with the hope that the flashes produced by exploding shells would enable him to adjust subsequent fire as required. As A Company reached Burntside House the gun crews lifted their fire – which, in the event, had failed to hit the house – and redirected it on the second target area. HMS *Arrow*, on whose heavy weight of fire so many in 2 Para depended, began her mission by firing star shells to help illuminate the battlefield. Although no light emerged from Burntside House and no fire originated from within, 3 Platoon took no chances and fired two 84mm Carl Gustav anti-armour missiles at the structure. The first round missed, while two further attempts ended in frustrating misfires, whereupon 2 Platoon sought the same result with rifle, machine-gun, and

66mm-rocket fire. Four civilians were inside but, lying on the floor, miraculously remained unscathed, despite a grenade exploding in one of the bedrooms. An Argentine platoon had indeed been present in the area, but had left either during or immediately prior to the assault. The position near the pond thought to contain tents nevertheless proved an error, although after the fighting two dead Argentines were found between the house and the pond.

With A Company's objective secure – and without casualties – Jones now ordered B Company to begin its advance. Maj. Crosland's men did not find it difficult to reach their start line, which required only that they follow a track leading south down a narrow section of land between Camilla Creek and Burntside Pond. Their start line stood only 100m from the Argentine position, a point chosen by the Patrols Platoon around midnight. B Company had arrived on time – no mean feat in darkness – but had to wait for A Company's attack first. In order to take advantage of the massive firepower available from *Arrow* – a 4.5in gun capable of firing twenty-five to thirty shells a minute – the Company FOO had to identify the desired target and then order its illumination, before HE rounds could be called in. But while the plan appeared simple enough, its execution failed on the basis of no visibility, the result of a combination of darkness and rain (not to mention the fact that radio communication initially failed) causing *Arrow* to fire star shells without a clear indication of the target's location, apart from the original grid reference. Once back on the net the NGFO announced that *Arrow* could no longer fire, the result of a mechanical failure in her turret – thus very prematurely ending the naval supporting fire upon which B Company expected to rely to aid its attack. Crosland had to press the attack nonetheless, with illumination only now theoretically available from the battalion's two mortars. The shortage of artillery would soon manifest itself when the FOO called for the 105mm guns to switch their targets from those forward of A Company to those facing B Company, a process which took some time since A Company had now

MIXED QUALITY OF BRITISH INTELLIGENCE

The assessment of the SAS that the troops on the isthmus were demoralised, hungry and numerically weak proved false. Fortunately, the two Recce Platoon patrols Jones dispatched on 27 May provided him with enough intelligence to appreciate this, though the patrols could not see as far as Darwin, much less Goose Green itself. At the colonel's commanding officer's 'O' group, Jones indicated that an Argentine infantry company was reported occupying Coronation Point; this was in fact not the case. Jones was aware that sixteen trenches were identified on the northern slope of the ridge about 650m west of Darwin inlet, but he surprisingly issued no orders to bombard this position, to deploy a smoke screen to mask A Company's advance or to assign a sub-unit to capture this point.

achieved its objective. Nevertheless, without illuminating rounds available, no light could be provided to B Company.

In the absence of this particular form of ordnance, the 105s fired on the best available grid reference, adjusting the fall of their shells according to the resulting flash and sound. Employing this unscientific but not altogether ineffective method, the guns continuously fired as B Company advanced; the shells dropping ahead of the troops in the manner of a 'creeping barrage', a tactic developed during the First World War. The men began their move at 0300 hrs, en route to their objective, Boca House, 5,000m distant. Crosland had devised a simple plan:

> My orders were clear – advance straight down the west side destroying all in the way … The company was tight and prickly, with two machine-guns or an M79 per section. We contained a lot of firepower. This was going to be a violent gutter fight, trench by trench – he who hit hardest won.
>
> (Adkin, *Goose Green*, pp. 188–9)

THE PITFALLS OF NIGHT-FIGHTING

When, before daylight, Major Crosland, B Company commander, was asked over the radio to identify his position, he admitted to having no idea: 'Four hundred yards west of the moon for all I knew'. The difficulties associated with making progress in the dark, and systematically clearing trenches, led to inevitable delay in executing the CO's complex plan, which required that B Company establish itself much closer to Boca House than it actually had by 0500 hrs, when Crosland began to organise the scattered elements of his company.

Employing machine-guns against the trenches, followed by grenades, Crosland's men maintained the momentum of the attack throughout, making early contact with their opponents. Three minutes after leaving their start line, the leading sections destroyed a machine-gun post as the whole company continued to move forward, clearing trenches as they advanced. Inevitably, B Company came under mortar and artillery fire and amidst the gloom it took forty-five minutes alone to clear an Argentine position containing mortars and anti-aircraft missiles, which B Company had bypassed on its flank. Thus, notwithstanding the problems inherent in trying to maintain their cohesion in darkness, with Argentine resistance relatively light B Company had made significant progress during this opening phase of the attack – and all without loss to themselves. The company carried forward, although the CO had no idea where he actually was. Around 0500 hrs he began the lengthy process so characteristic of night actions, of reorganising and reassembling his men in preparation for their continued advance toward Boca House.

Nevertheless, Jones' plan had fallen considerably behind schedule. Maj. Neame's D Company, to be discussed shortly, was meant by this time to have reached the knoll near Camilla Creek, while Farrar-Hockley's A Company, to be discussed later, was supposed to have reached Coronation Point and gone into reserve. A Company had in fact met no resistance, but both B and D Companies had been held up by Manresa's men, eating into the time allotted by Jones for the achievement of each objective.

The Advance on Boca House and Darwin Ridge

28 May

0500 hrs	After trench-clearing, B Company begins to reassemble its scattered elements before resuming its advance on Boca House; with A and B Companies' progress delayed as a result of resistance at Darwin Ridge and Boca House, respectively, Jones orders D Company, meant to act in reserve, to move forward in support of B Company
0520 hrs	A Company reaches southern end of Coronation Point and finds it unoccupied
0630 hrs	(Dawn). A Company pinned by heavy Argentine fire at gorse gully; 2 Para has advanced only halfway to Goose Green, whereas Jones had calculated for the entire action to cease around this time; fighting henceforth proceeds in daylight
0700 hrs	Approximate beginning of fight for Darwin Hill; A Company is stuck in gorse gully for at least two hours
0725 hrs	A Company requests Harrier airstrike against Argentine trenches on Darwin Ridge, but is refused on grounds of poor flying conditions at sea
0800 hrs	Two Pucaras attack area around Camilla Creek House with rockets but fail to hit the 105mm guns nearby; Support Company, initially on a peninsula west of the isthmus, moves to centre of isthmus
0830 hrs	Jones, anxious to examine the circumstances responsible for holding up A Company's progress, reaches Farrar-Hockley's position
0900 hrs	A small group from A Company, including Farrar-Hockley, charge up the slope of Darwin Hill, but is repulsed; Support Company situated 1,200m north of Darwin Ridge

28 May	0930 hrs	Jones, after being present with A Company for sixty minutes, and anxious to break the impasse at Darwin Hill, charges up the gorse gully on his own and is mortally wounded; Sgt Blackburn reports 'Sunray is down' one minute later; Keeble assumes command of 2 Para; C Company (Jenner), initially pinned down, advances down centre of isthmus under heavy fire in support of A Company; D Company continues to support B Company on western end of Argentine defensive line
	1045 hrs	Two Scout helicopters fly south to Camilla Creek House in a casualty evacuation (Casevac) role; one is shot down at c. 1100 hrs, the other returns empty

By sunrise 2 Para still had a good deal of ground yet to take; Jones' timings were completely out, with most of the objectives for the early phases of his plan not yet achieved, and from the time since A Company had begun its advance the battalion stood only halfway to Goose Green. The unit now faced ten hours of daylight ahead of it, with totally bare ground to its front, most of it occupied by forces well dug in.

Meanwhile, Lt Col Piaggi had recognised, even before Farrar-Hockley's men began to approach his main defensive line, that an opportunity presented itself to mount a counter-attack, particularly in light of Manresa's withdrawal in defiance of orders. With some sort of response to the British offensive in mind, Piaggi had been in contact with his superiors in Stanley, requesting support. Reinforcements and air strikes would materialise in due course, his superiors informed him, so long as the weather permitted helicopters to operate; but he was for the moment to content himself with simply holding his ground. In light of the absence of any available assistance from beyond the isthmus, Piaggi ordered 2nd Lt Aliaga's platoon from 8th Regiment to move from the area just south of Boca House and proceed north, to occupy the largely empty trenches on the far left of the main defensive line just south and south-east of the ruins of Boca House. Piaggi also ordered

B Company's position at first light: highly vulnerable and exposed.

Lt Estevez and his platoon, deployed in reserve near Goose Green, to shift north and counter-attack, thus providing help to Manresa.

This platoon possessed no training in counter-attacking and he had no support from artillery; in any event the guns were running short of ammunition. Estevez could, however, bolster Manresa's defence by deploying his machine-guns. Accordingly, Estevez proceeded north, passing over the gorse line until he reached Pelufo's platoon on the ridge to the west of Darwin. Estevez did not, in the event, carry on to assist Manresa's A Company, for Pelufo objected, claiming he needed reinforcements to remedy his own precarious position at a time when a counter-attack, carried out in darkness, was impossible – as well as pointless – in light of the withdrawal of Manresa's company then already underway. Estevez concurred, and instead positioned his platoon in the trenches on Pelufo's right. This made eminent sense, and yet, for the moment at least, Darwin Hill remained unoccupied, together with the gully between it and a ridge running north-west, and it will be recalled that upon this ridge, occupied by Estevez and Pelufo, stood the main Argentine defensive position.

These positions were held by approximately 200 Argentines drawn from formations under Aliaga on the left, Pelufo in the centre, and Estevez on the right, plus elements of Manresa's company, which had retreated from further north. No proper cohesion existed within this composite unit, for all three platoons belonged to different regiments. With no overall commander, this role belonged by default to Manresa, who had no time in which

FIRE AND MANOEUVRE

At Goose Green, the mechanics of 2 Para's platoon attack generally involved two sections forward and one in reserve. When under exceptionally heavy fire and lacking a way forward, some men were forced to ground for long periods, while others able to make progress generally knelt to fire between spurts of movement, with covering fire offered by others – a process then reciprocated as the sub-unit advanced. During the pre-dawn phases of the battle, pitch-black darkness often obliged the paras to close to within 20–40m of the defenders before the former could perceive a viable target to engage. From time to time, particularly in the dark, a company commander found it necessary as a prerequisite to any further advance to reorganise his men, which entailed gathering them together from their dispersed positions by firing flares into the air or shouting for everyone to converge on the officer concerned.

to draw up a proper plan of defence. Indeed, having only returned to the position just before dawn, Manresa was not even aware of the composition of the forces now under his command. Still, with the British clearly visible in the gathering light and with open ground stretching before them – so facilitating fire at long range – even unsteady infantry were likely to be able to maintain fire from entrenched positions, which they had prepared over the preceding weeks. After all, 2 Para's journey south had taken seven weeks.

Meanwhile, D Company, acting as the reserve and the last of the four companies into action, proceeded from its assembly area at Camilla Creek House towards its start line, losing its way in the blackness. Nevertheless, this was eventually put to rights, and D Company would soon encounter a series of trenches held by part of Manresa's company meant to be confronted by Crosland's men. Thus, in the confusion caused by darkness and poor timings, D Company now found itself ahead of B Company, poised to take on the right and rear of Manresa's formation.

Jones' original plan was going awry – hence his decision around 0500 hrs to push D Company forward to make up for lost time. He had originally envisaged the battalion reaching the outskirts of both settlements around 0600 hrs – only sixty minutes away. But with precious time lost in B Company's reassembling its scattered elements – a process that was taking longer than actually expelling the defenders from their positions – he needed to accelerate the pace of progress. Thus far, 2 Para had crossed 1,500m of ground; but another third of that distance remained, and Piaggi's main defensive position had yet to be reached. D Company soon came under fire, with tracer filling the air, but not before it had reached as near as 30 or 40m from the Argentine firing line, which inflicted 2 Para's first casualties of the battle, one of them a mortal wound. Argentine mortar fire now began to descend, adding another two casualties: one soldier shot through the head and killed, the other suffering a shattered hip when a round burst his water bottle.

Since 0330 hrs, A Company had remained motionless west of Burntside House, but an hour later Farrar-Hockley received an order over the radio to resume the advance – now with the support of artillery, which had shifted periodically to assist other companies in light of the malfunction aboard *Arrow*. His objective was Coronation Point, 1,000m away, though a track and a fence could both be conveniently used to help navigate the company through the cold, wet and darkness. By 0445 hrs A Company now constituted the leading company, while the others continued to regroup to the west. Strangely, Farrar-Hockley did not initially encounter any opposition, although he expected to confront a series of defended trenches. This was a logical conclusion, given the previous experience of other companies. Thus, by the time A Company reached the northern edge of Darwin inlet at 0520 hrs, it stood within 500m of the settlement itself, which lay just across the water.

Throughout this phase, and indeed for the remainder of the action, 2 Para found itself woefully short of mortar support.

These two weapons, handled by Mortar Platoon, moved around the field and kept in radio contact with Tac 1, battalion HQ. The rifle companies could call for supporting mortar fire through their respective Mortar Platoon NCOs who acted as observers, but there were no helicopters to ferry the bombs from the original baseplate position near Camilla Creek House. Thus, when the two mortars moved forward before dawn there were no helicopters available to ferry the ammunition forward, forcing the men of the Mortar Platoon to carry it at a rate of eight bombs each – an inefficient and exhausting method. This led to a shortage of ammunition, with a particular lack of illuminating rounds, since the battalion was meant to depend on the star shells fired from *Arrow*. Moreover, the first new baseplate position was found to be too soft to permit fire, obliging the mortarmen to establish themselves on harder, though exposed ground.

Acute shortage of helicopter lift

During the battle, Sea King helicopters conveyed mortar bombs to the original baseplate position near the battalion RV at Camilla Creek House and then ferried more by employing a captured Land Rover. Heavily laden with bombs on the outward journey, the Land Rover then ferried casualties back, just as helicopters shifted ammunition forward and collected the wounded on their return journey. Had 2 Para not had the fortuitous advantage of this vehicle, virtually no mortar bombs would have been moved forward during the battle because 2 Para's Land Rovers were still sitting aboard ship. Since the battle was supposed to be virtually over by dawn, no one had planned to use Sea Kings or Gazelles to ferry ammunition forward, though in the event a limited number did.

On reaching Coronation Point at 0520 hrs, A Company discovered it was unoccupied. Thus far, Farrar-Hockley had sustained no casualties, sunrise was not due for more than an hour and Darwin Hill stood only 1,000m away. If A Company continued to make progress at this rate, it was likely it would reach that feature, which overlooked the settlement, by first light. This would conform to the CO's plan, since Jones wanted A Company to capture the settlement when the sun was up. But the timetable came to a juddering halt, for Farrar-Hockley waited an hour before resuming his advance, owing to the fact that A Company, now in control of Coronation Point, was much further advanced in its progress than B and D. When he radioed for authority to move ahead, Farrar-Hockley was told to await the CO's presence, for Jones would not allow his plan to be altered without his own assessment of the situation. It seemed odd that the Argentines had chosen not to defend Coronation Point, leaving the eastern side of the isthmus virtually undefended compared with the centre and west. Jones' decision to see matters for himself may have been sound, but of course the time required for him to arrive on the scene caused further delay to A Company's progress. After reviewing Farrar-Hockley's position, Jones ordered his rapid advance, in so doing gaining ground where the other rifle companies had not. By this time it was nearly dawn, so all possible speed was required to reach the settlement before light exposed A Company to any defenders on the eastern side of the isthmus. Accordingly, the lead platoon advanced down the gorse-covered gully that approached Darwin Hill, from which Darwin could be easily seen together with, beyond it, the airstrip and Goose Green.

A Company now began to cross open ground in a gorse gully towards Darwin Hill, with a view to reaching high ground and acquiring for itself a clear view of the settlement. From this position, and with one platoon providing supporting fire from the causeway, the settlement was very likely to fall. Light now began to emerge along the horizon, highlighting the fact that the ground lay totally open, covered only by grassy hummocks,

MEDICAL AID ON THE BATTLEFIELD

Aboard *Norland*, 2 Para paid particular attention to the question of caring for casualties. Keeble, the 2ic, appreciated that if helicopters could not readily evacuate the wounded, moving men by *ad hoc* means to the regimental aid post would prove very slow and thus endanger their lives. He therefore emphasised the need for battlefield resuscitation in substitution for mere first aid administered where a man fell. The battalion's Medical Officer, Captain Stephen Hughes, took aboard 1,000 drips for intravenous infusion to offset blood loss, with each paratrooper issued with, and taught how to use, an IV to accompany the standard issue morphine and shell dressings. This training, as well as other vital medical instruction, was designed to allow soldiers to leave wounded men behind with a reasonable prospect of survival until such time as they could be properly evacuated.

irregular in shape and difficult for one's footing – the treacherous 'babies' heads'. Darwin Hill was low, with a gully to its left filled with high gorse, and to the left of the lower slope of Darwin stood the opening of a re-entrant. Then, at 0630 hrs, A Company took heavy machine-gun fire, obliging it to take whatever cover it could find. One section rushed for the re-entrant, defended by Estevez's platoon, which wounded two paras in the growing light and forced the section to return to the gorse gully. Several others fell wounded there but, in general, the Argentines fired high and failed to inflict the sort of heavy casualties likely in a frontal assault over bare ground. Private Martin of 1 Platoon described the experience of being pinned down:

I was at the back of the platoon with part of company headquarters. When firing started we doubled forward a bit, went to ground, and opened fire on the hill. We were soon under mortar fire as well but were saved by the soft ground. One man got hit going forward to the left. It was all chaos with no orders

as the section commander had gone into the gully. Gradually we
made our way down to the beach by the water [the inlet].

(Adkin, *Goose Green*, p. 225)

This rather overly pessimistic assessment belied the fact that
Farrar-Hockley was not facing any enemy on the face of Darwin
Hill, which overlooked the gully, otherwise rendering the attack
a very costly one. Men of A Company proceeded to attack
trenches situated on a spur to the right of the gully entrance using
grenades, 66mms and a GPMG, but engaging the Argentines at
close range denied the paras the benefit of supporting artillery fire
since incoming shells could strike friendly forces. The paras quite
naturally attempted to execute a left flanking movement around
the spur, but heavy machine-gun fire rendered this impossible,
with one man wounded in that instance and another during an
attempt up the left side of the gully, where rounds whizzing just
above the ground began to set fire to the gorse.

A Company had encountered only a portion of the fourteen
or more bunkers and trenches stretching across the isthmus, and
high explosive rounds from supporting mortar fire largely proved
themselves substantially ineffective, burying themselves in the soft
ground and causing little damage. Still, at least the limited supply
of white phosphorus rounds could provide bright flashes of light
and smoke, masking A Company's advance in a limited fashion.
All the while, Argentine mortar fire continued to rain down,
aiding the defenders in holding their dominating ground while
A Company, spread too thinly, could not concentrate sufficient
firepower to drive them off. In short, the action in the gorse gully
had degenerated into a series of uncoordinated movements and
small-scale attacks carried out by sections and individual soldiers –
with nothing but casualties to show for it.

Quite sensibly, Farrar-Hockley deployed considerable firepower
with GPMGs, but he had no artillery fire in support so long as the
guns continued to direct their fire missions against those Argentine
positions which were impeding B Company's efforts to take Boca

WHITE PHOSPHORUS MORTAR ROUNDS

To offset the problem of mortar bombs sinking into the soft ground before exploding, the British sometimes fired white phosphorus (WP) rounds from their 81mm mortars, since unlike their high-explosive counterparts, they continued to burn even against strenuous efforts to extinguish them. The Paras also used WP grenades for trench-clearing.

House. When at last A Company did receive some support from the guns they soon went silent, as FOOs began to appreciate the very real risks of putting down fire with the Argentines so close to both companies. Moreover, HMS *Arrow* had left the area, her gun still jammed. This left Farrar-Hockley with the final option: to call in a Harrier strike, which he did at 0725 hrs, aware that their cluster bombs could wreak devastation on the trenches stretching across the open ridge. Yet when his request reached the aircraft carriers, he received a refusal: foggy conditions rendered take-off (and landing) impossible. A Company had now reached an impasse: the guns were supporting B Company, which needed them for their advance against Boca House; naval gunfire was unavailable; aircraft could not fly owing to adverse weather conditions; and only two mortars were available, and these were incapable of laying down sufficient firepower to produce the results required. In addition, the defenders enjoyed a clear field of fire for much of the approach, forcing Farrar-Hockley's men to huddle in what dead ground they could, which thus far now accounted for a frustrating ninety minutes. An option, as yet untried, now presented itself: A Company could make recourse to the difficult business of neutralising trenches in succession with 66mms and grenades. This was a slow process which offered some hope of making up for lost time; A Company had already been held up well beyond Col Jones' timetable.

Jones, of course, now long aware of A Company's difficulties in getting forward, was growing increasingly angry and frustrated.

For no sooner had the sun come up than both A and B Companies had been stalled on reaching the main Argentine defence position – A at Darwin Hill and B near Boca House. This situation was exacerbated by the ineffective fire of his guns and his staff's ignorance of the Argentines' dug-in positions. Compounding Jones' problems, shells continued to rain down, yet he could direct no counter-battery fire or air assets against the three guns firing from unidentified positions. This left 2 Para to cope almost entirely on its own, leaving its CO to find a solution to the deadlock.

As Jones adhered to the philosophy that an officer, whatever his rank, must lead from the front, that is precisely what he resolved to do. On the other hand, most officers agree that the place of a CO is well behind the frontline, in a position to observe, appreciate 'the bigger picture', analyse the situation, devise a plan and issue orders accordingly – as opposed to maintaining a physical presence in the midst of the action where he cannot influence events except at a very local level. This sort of micro-management

Debris left after the fighting on Mount Longdon. After the war a specialist disposal unit of the Royal Engineers made safe and cleared away vast amounts of weapons and ordnance.

style of leadership, many contend, constitutes the responsibility of the company and platoon but, above all, the section commanders. By contrast, even as a battalion commanding officer, Jones believed he must observe events personally, assess the situation and take a personal hand in the outcome of his decisions. In this way, he could impose his will upon a given situation and thus lead by example. As Farrar-Hockley reported that intense Argentine fire was pinning his men down and holding up the advance, Jones felt he must reverse his fortunes – an objective requiring his presence in no less than the frontline.

In the critical situation confronting Jones, he could not break the deadlock by introducing greater firepower: he had none to add. Neither air strikes nor naval gunfire were available, artillery was in short supply and most of the unit's heavy weapons were not present on the battlefield, apart from the Milans and machine-guns available from Support Company, still uncommitted in the rear. While he had the option of committing reserves to break the deadlock in the form of C or D Companies, Jones decided to break the impasse by inspiring and encouraging his men forward in the style so tragically characteristic of the exploits performed in no-man's-land during the First World War. In short, he headed for the gorse gully with Tac 1, which consisted of a dozen men, and found what little cover there was to be had while small arms and machine-guns rattled away, and artillery and mortar fire continued to rain down on the positions held by A, B and D Companies.

By radio, Jones, now in the gorse gully 500m north-east of A Company's position and 1,000m east of B Company's, instructed Farrar-Hockley to press on. About this time, Pucaras appeared and fired on the guns and Camilla Creek House. At about the same time, 2 Para's two mortars now came into action, but with insufficient weight of fire and not enough mortar bombs to hand. The three guns continued to fire in support of B Company, shifting their guns later to help A Company – but often inaccurately owing to difficulties for the FOOs in observing the fall of shells and the prevalence of strong winds. D Company meanwhile stood in reserve, at this point situated on a ridge 700m due north of Jones' position. Neame received precise instructions not to move forward, but by radio he offered the suggestion of a right-flanking move along the shoreline. Jones cut him short, brusquely telling him to get off the net and not interfere in the CO's conduct of the battle. At the same time, C Company (Jenner) was advancing down the axis track, just east of D Company, approaching the gently elevated ground west of Coronation Point. Jenner offered to deploy his light machine-guns to assist in supporting Farrar-Hockley, still pinned in the open facing Darwin Hill as daylight gathered. Again, Jones intervened, this time addressing the C Company 2ic, Lt Peter Kennedy, to stay off the net – bluntly asserting that he desired no interference while he sought to sort out the problem.

Significantly, Jones took an hour to determine his next course of action. He got on the net to Neame and urged action. Sgt Norman, Jones' bodyguard, described the circumstances:

> A Company's attack started floundering after they cleared up the Argentine first platoon position. The CO got on the radio and told them to get a grip, speed up and continue the movement, which they couldn't. So he said: 'I'm not having any of this', and decided to go up and join A Company. To say he got a little pear-shaped would be an understatement. When he made up his mind that a thing was going to be done then it was going to be done, and off he went all the way round the edge of the inlet.

(Adkin, *Goose Green*, p. 240)

Rather than commit his reserve too early, without Support Company yet on the field, and frustrated by the ineffectiveness of the guns and mortars, the CO decided to make a dash forward himself. At about 0830 hrs he ran forward towards the gorse gully, produced a smoke screen with WP grenades, and came within 200m of A Company's position, outpacing the rest of his tactical headquarters in the process. He found Farrar-Hockley, by which time A Company had cleared about seven trenches on the western side of the spur. Other Argentine positions further west, however, continued to issue fire across the top of the spur with such violence that A Company's continued efforts to skirt round the spur or to approach it frontally failed. No progress from the gully, it seemed, could be made with GPMG fire alone; Farrar-Hockley needed artillery or, even more effective, aircraft, to break the impasse. Argentine artillery had now set fire to much of the gorse, not far from where Jones hugged the ground with Tac 1, and Farrar-Hockley and staff, around him. D Company, meanwhile, had reached the western side of the isthmus and now stood 300m from the water. Neame got on the radio and suggested his company make an attempt to outflank the Argentine line by skirting it along the shore. This, he reckoned, would break the deadlock involving A and B Companies and turn the whole Argentine position on the ridge. 'Don't tell me how to run my battle!' came Jones' caustic reply.

At about 0900 hrs Support Company reached a position around 1,200m from Darwin Ridge, bearing its Milans and machine-guns, but with instructions to remain *in situ*; unaccountably, Jones turned down a suggestion that the Milans come forward. The colonel wanted A Company to achieve the breakthrough unassisted, driving off the Argentine defenders in the middle of the ridge. While A Company was making forward movement only very gradually, it was clear that the schedule Jones had outlined at his 'O' group the previous day was now irrelevant, with the battalion two and a half hours behind schedule as a consequence of resistance offered to A and B Companies. If the Argentines had chosen to counter-attack at this point, they might very well have either driven 2 Para back, or in any event compromised any further progress. A Company in particular stood in a vulnerable predicament in front of Darwin Hill. Before Piaggi lay a generous window of opportunity, stretching from about 0730 hrs until as late as noon; it remained to be seen if he would act upon it.

At about 0900 hrs the mortars ran out of ammunition and a small group from A Company, including Farrar-Hockley, ran up towards the spur of Darwin Hill. This resulted in three para deaths and their repulse, for the defenders swept the top with a withering fire. At this point, it appears Jones believed that he could alter the situation by moving ahead himself around the right of the spur and towards the closest trenches. At about 0930 hrs he duly ran forward, shouting 'Follow me!', shortly after which he fell from a single shot. Sgt Norman was the first to arrive on the scene to assist him, with others following, including Sgt Blackburn, also from Tac 1, who radioed the 2ic, Maj. Keeble, the coded message, 'Sunray is down'. After being carried on a makeshift stretcher to a spot deemed suitable as a helicopter-landing site, from which to evacuate him to the regimental aid post (RAP) for urgent medical attention, Lt Col Jones died. Forty-five minutes later, two Scout helicopters flew forward from Camilla Creek House in a casevac role, but Pucaras appeared and shot one of them down with its 7.62mm machine-gun, killing the pilot and badly injuring the crewman. The other Scout returned to Camilla Creek House without any injured – or the CO's body.

A Company meanwhile continued to make slow progress, though deploying its 66mm rockets to good effect against bunkers and trenches, causing the occupants of various trenches to throw up their hands in surrender about fifteen minutes after Jones

Looking down the re-entrant which Lt Col Jones charged as seen from the Argentine position. The CO was hit by a single shot fired from a command bunker which is thought to have been destroyed shortly thereafter by a 66mm rocket fired by Cpl Dave Abols of A Company.

Jones' mortal wound

It was in the course of his attempt to achieve a breakthrough of the Argentine main defensive position that Lt Col Jones received a single round from an Argentine machine-gunner, probably from Lt Roberto Estevez's platoon of 12th Regtiment. Dr Rick Jolly recollected that: 'The entry wound was about 8mm in diameter, and just behind his right collarbone, but there was a much larger exit wound down the left side of his lower abdomen … The bullet, having penetrated the apex of his right lung, passed behind his heart, bounced off the lower end of the thoracic spine and crossed the midline. It exited halfway between the naval and crest of 'H''s left hip, still possessing considerable kinetic energy … In my heart of hearts, I do not think that 'H' would have survived in the end.' (Ramsey, *The Falklands War Then and Now*, p. 305)

was shot. Farrar-Hockley's men discovered twenty-three trenches on the central part of the ridge, of whose occupants nearly twenty lay dead and twice that number wounded. A Company suffered six dead in the attack on the gorse gully and the spur, plus eleven wounded – a one-in-five casualty rate. The extent to which Jones' solo charge had broken the deadlock has been the source of controversy ever since, but it is relevant to state that no one but Sgt Norman was within easy reach of him when he charged, with only a few personnel from Tac 1 some distance behind. In this respect, he did not personally carry any elements of A Company with him, or at that immediate moment inspire their forward movement, as none of the company's personnel were aware of Jones' dash. He had not sought to take any soldiers with him and Farrar-Hockley was not aware of his movement. That said, the company commander's judgement on this matter has a great deal to commend it:

It cannot be said that 'H''s courageous sortie – or whatever he had in mind – inspired the soldiers at that moment, because few, if any, were aware of what he was doing. But his enterprise on our right did distract the enemy there to one degree or another. I do not agree that a particular piece of ground was taken on this account. Most important was 'H''s standing and drive in the Battalion. He put us to a difficult task; he inspired us in the undertaking; he was up front from the beginning and hence provided the dynamic needs for the impetus of attacking and continuing to attack until we had succeeded. His inspiration and example were to remain with us for the rest of the campaign.

(Adkin, *Goose Green*, p. 254)

B Company's Attack on Boca House

When the sun inched over the horizon around 0630 hrs, B Company still remained held up in their advance on Boca House, with the emerging light promising to render their reception all the more unpleasant. Crosland later assessed the situation:

At daybreak the enemy could sit back in bunkers and engage us at a range of 900–1,440 metres with guns, mortars, heavy machine-guns and snipers. The ground was very similar to Salisbury Plain [i.e. flat] and we found ourselves grovelling at the base of a hill not dissimilar to Bowls Barrow. Here we fought and grovelled for nearly seven hours.

(Adkin, *Goose Green*, p. 255)

At about 0800 hrs two Pucaras, flying out of Stanley – all others had been withdrawn from the airfield at Goose Green before the battle – attacked Camilla Creek House with rockets and then proceeded towards the gun position, missing their target and only just dodging Blowpipe guided missiles, before returning to Stanley. Three hours later two more arrived over Camilla Creek House, shooting down a helicopter with cannon- and machine-gun fire and killing the pilot, while the second one successfully evaded destruction. One of the Pucaras crashed into Blue

B Company's line of advance, showing the remains of Boca House. Opposition encountered in and around the structure's foundations by Crosland's A Company, as well as on the 15m (50ft) hill behind them, confounded Lt Col Jones' precisely timed schedule by many hours.

Mountain when the pilot got lost owing to poor visibility; the other reached Stanley safely.

Meanwhile, B Company faced stiff opposition opposite Boca House, especially now that the sun was up. Even the new recruits amongst the defenders could and did put up a respectable fight, with a clear field of fire available for several hundred metres, no threat from the air and very little from guns and mortars. The latter ran short of ammunition, leaving the paras with no proper smokescreen with which to mask their advance in the clear light of day. Moreover, the soft ground absorbed much of the explosive power of the bombs and only a lucky, direct hit on a trench would result in any serious damage to the defenders. Progress was actually only achieved with direct fire weapons, especially Milans fired against bunkers, but 2 Para's observers still could not identify the location of the Argentine guns – three 105mm pack howitzers deployed on the northern edge of Goose Green. These were well concealed, and with no British aircraft over the battlefield at this stage, the attackers had no hope of silencing them. Similarly, the mortars placed on the outskirts of Goose Green, on a small peninsula east of the settlement, continued to fire with impunity, their locations as yet unknown to the British. In the meantime, Piaggi had been demanding reinforcements from Parada for hours, but to no avail. This may have accounted for the former's failure to launch a counter-attack, or perhaps he felt that his ill-trained men could not muster the means to conduct one.

It should be observed that Boca House, B Company's objective, was in fact not a house at all, but merely the foundations of a structure no longer standing, and thus the position not only offered no visible point of recognition, but could furnish no protection to a defender. In this area, the Argentines had deployed troops under 2nd Lt Pelufo and Aliaga on slightly elevated ground on the western side of the isthmus, south-east of the ruins. These, in turn, formed part of Manresa's command. As B Company approached, the defenders offered a brisk fire from rifles, machine-guns and mortars, bringing the advance to a

B Company's line of advance. Major Crosland's company moved from its start line at around 0320 hrs and proceeded along the extreme west side of the isthmus, only meeting strong opposition when it approached Boca House, which lies due west of Darwin.

halt – but leaving no option to retire, either – and obliging many of Crosland's men to take what little cover they could from the gorse line just north of the Boca House position. Still, resistance on the west end of the line began to break just before 1200 hrs as the paras of B Company attempted to outflank the position along the beach, employing Milans to good effect as they did so. Some took advantage of the scarce little cover available from the gorse line just north of Boca House, together with elements from D Company and Support Company nearby. At last, at midday, Boca House, and the 15m (50ft) hill south of it, fell, almost exactly as A Company broke through Darwin Ridge and crushed resistance there, leaving the Argentine main defensive position in tatters.

Some time between 0930 and 1000 hrs, Major Chris Keeble learned with dismay that the CO was dead, devolving command on him, a circumstance complicated by the fact that he lay 1,500m away from the CO's position at Battalion HQ. Time was also required to ascertain the situation from the two forward companies, A and B, for without this he could not make a decision on the use of reserves. Keeble later described his decision-making process at this critical juncture:

> A Company's battle around Darwin sounded a shambles and the ground favoured the defence there. There was little point in reinforcing failure. B Company with Johnny Crosland, on the other hand, were in a reasonable position, despite being pinned down, and so I told him to assume command until I could get forward with Major Hector Gulan, the ubiquitous and invaluable Brigade Liaison Officer, who had a direct line to Brigadier Julian Thompson.

> (Arthur, *Above All, Courage*, p. 192)

At 1045 hrs Keeble and his staff started down the track towards Crosland's B Company, which they did not reach until sometime after 1100 hrs. There was still no possibility of assistance from Harriers owing to poor weather out to sea and, with other units of

The remains of an enemy position at Goose Green. The Argentines dug over twenty trenches across the isthmus, together with bunkers, on the basis that any attacker would almost certainly approach from the north. Mines laid at various points along the beaches served to discourage the amphibious alternative.

3 Commando Brigade on their way east, Keeble could not expect any reinforcements. Nevertheless, all were confident of success and despite the loss of their CO there was never any question but that the paras, for whom attaining the mission is always paramount, would continue to prosecute the attack.

SUPPORT COMPANY'S FRUSTRATIONS

While the rifle companies made good progress during the pre-dawn hours of 28 May, Support Company experienced a host of problems. They sought to consolidate at a fire support base on the flank, necessitating the carrying of a considerable amount of heavy weapons and ammunition, such that when the fighting began only the Machine Gun Platoon stood in a position to lend its support. In the darkness the snipers and Milan teams were blind, leaving the rifle companies, already operating without the aid of HMS *Arrow*'s gun, to engage without much hoped-for fire support.

By the time Keeble reached B Company around midday, the situation for 2 Para had undergone a remarkable turn for the better: A Company stood in possession of the gorse gully and spur, where the Argentines there had surrendered, leaving the whole of the eastern end of their main defence line neutralised. B Company had used Milans as 'bunker-busters', in skilful combination with GPMGs, while Neame's D Company had outflanked the Argentine position along the beach at the extreme west, with rocks partly covering its advance and the area mercifully free of mines. This development, in turn, established it in a position also to present flanking fire with Milans and machine-guns against the trenches on Darwin Ridge, precipitating capitulations there. Thus, between the close-quarter fighting by A Company in the gorse gully and the efforts of B and D Companies further west, aided by effective use of heavy weapons and a flanking movement, 2 Para achieved the required breakthrough. This resulted in twelve dead and fifteen prisoners from Aliaga's platoon; a handful escaped towards the airfield and most of the rest were taken unhurt.

Now, just after midday, almost ten hours after the fighting had begun and five and a half since dawn, 2 Para had finally overcome the main Argentine positions. According to Jones' original plan, the battle ought to have ended with the capture of Goose Green hours ago; but there was still much fighting left to be done – all in the cold light of day.

Final Objectives: Goose Green Airfield and School

28 May		
	1130 hrs	One company of Argentine reinforcements dispatched from Stanley arrives south of Goose Green to aid Piaggi
	1200 hrs	B and D Companies outflank Argentine position on extreme western side of the isthmus, B Company taking Boca House and 15m (50ft) hill behind it and D Company providing supporting flanking fire to A Company, which succeeds in breaking main defensive line along Darwin Ridge
	1215 hrs	C Company, situated at the gorse line, advances south, eventually towards the school just north of Goose Green; D Company, further west, also begins advance against both airfield and school; B Company proceeds further south along west coast before swinging east beyond the airfield
	1300 hrs	Elements of C and D Companies commence attack on school
	1500 hrs	Two Aeromacchis, followed shortly thereafter by two Pucaras, attack B and D Company's positions with napalm, but inflict no casualties; two aircraft shot down; fighting around airfield and school slackens
	1530 hrs	Three Harriers fail to neutralise 35mm guns on Goose Green peninsula
	1550 hrs	Combat Team Solari (132 officers and men) plus a 105mm recoilless gun and one 81mm mortar moves from Stanley to Goose Green by helicopter

Although Piaggi had been requesting reinforcements from Stanley for hours, none were despatched until 1100 hrs in the form of eighty-four men under First Lieutenant (1st Lt) Estoban arriving in nine helicopters. Their thirty-minute, 90km (56 miles) journey along the south coast took them up Choiseul Sound to touch down

POOR CO-ORDINATION OF SUPPLIES

The threat from Pucara aircraft kept British light helicopters from flying to forward areas of the battlefield until the afternoon, a problem exacerbated by the fact that there might have been better co-ordination of ammunition resupply and helicopter lift from HQ Company. Moreover, not only did heavy-lift helicopters not always bring the needed bulk ammunition to Camilla Creek House whence Scouts and Gazelles could carry it forward, the procedure for ordering up helicopters from Brigade HQ did not always succeed in producing a Sea King or other machine at the right time and place.

immediately south of Goose Green. With the fall of Darwin Ridge and the area around Boca House, Piaggi's position was contracting to include an area covering the airfield, about 1,400m south of the gorse line; the school, which sat at the head of an estuary with a bridge across it; and Goose Green settlement. The key to this area's capture was the school, through which ran a shoreline track and, east of the airstrip, an area designated the 'flagpole position' – a simple flag flying from a mast on high ground – which, owing to its position, dominated a track extending north–south. If 2 Para approached via this track they would have to capture both the flagpole position and the school to reach Goose Green; sub-units which proceeded south to capture the flagpole position would need to seize, or at least neutralise fire from, the school to prevent flanking fire reaching them from a distance of only 300m.

Piaggi, aware of his predicament, did not sit idle: he sent Lt Vasquez to reinforce the school, adding some of Estoban's recently arrived men to do so, while Estoban, for his part, busied himself gathering a couple of hundred air force personnel to assume a ground role to defend the settlement. In addition, a platoon from C Company 25th Regiment under Lt Centurion arrived at the airfield and flagpole position to strengthen the defence there.

Despite the collapse of their defensive position further north, Argentine fortunes appeared to be recovering, for the intervening ground extending south from Darwin Ridge to the airfield and the school was virtually flat, furnishing the defenders with excellent fields of fire. Several bunkers dotted the area around the airfield plus, just to the south, six 20mm anti-aircraft guns capable of serving in a ground role could offer devastating fire to a range of 2,000m, with a staggering rate of fire of 1,000 rounds a minute. In addition, two platoons from C Company 12th Regiment stood west and south of Goose Green, with the third platoon isolated at the southern end of the isthmus, shifted earlier by helicopter under the mistaken impression that a British landing threatened Piaggi from the rear. Lacking a radio and bearing no orders to influence events further north, it took no part in the fighting.

Around Goose Green itself, Piaggi maintained the residents in the community centre, with the buildings surrounded by bunkers and mortar positions; this deployment successfully deterred the attackers from firing into the settlement in the course of the battle. Other prominent features of the defence included the two Oerlikon anti-aircraft guns, positioned just east of the settlement on the peninsula, which juts out into Choiseul Sound. Like those deployed near the airfield, these guns could be used to fire horizontally against ground troops and enjoyed a range of 1,000m.

Keeble was determined to maintain the momentum of the attack following the breakthrough at Boca House and Darwin Ridge. So long as the Argentines could be kept under pressure, the prospect of victory loomed large for 2 Para, despite the presence of defences around the airfield and schoolhouse. In this last phase of the battle, Keeble directed A Company into reserve on Darwin Hill – the taking of the settlement itself, which was not occupied, could occur later. B Company was instructed to advance south along the western side of the isthmus and move past the airfield, before finally shifting east in a wide arc, taking it to the coast south of the settlement. Roger Jenner's C Company was to move against the airfield and Neame's D Company was to take the school and establish itself just outside the settlement itself. Keeble's plan meant that all rifle companies would be simultaneously on the advance, including one platoon from A Company detached to Jenner's formation, leaving Farrar-Hockley's other two platoons on Darwin Hill. Keeble wished to keep the Argentines under pressure, capture the airfield and envelop Goose Green – that is clear – but the various companies would have to cross, depending on their particular route, between 1,000 and 2,000m of completely open ground, which, if the Argentines chose to defend with any degree of determination, could prove costly. 2 Para still had poor indirect fire support in terms of mortars and artillery, and still awaited the massive firepower offered by air assets. Keeble's worries also extended to the problems inherent in fighting within a confined area, for with all the rifle companies on the move across it, they faced the genuine risk of intermingling, so disrupting the momentum of attack as a result of the ensuing confusion and increasing the risk of direct fire support weapons accidentally inflicting casualties on friendly troops.

Shortly after midday, C Company and the attached platoon from A Company, with fixed bayonets, began its move to cover the 1,500m to the airfield, the whole area completely bereft of cover. D Company unexpectedly crossed in front of it, demonstrating the danger of so many rifle companies operating in such a small area. The sight proved an inviting one for the crews of the 20mm anti-aircraft guns, backed by mortars and heavy machine-guns, and all enjoying a perfect view of their assailants who lacked the benefit of supporting fire, much less smoke to conceal their movement, as they advanced in open order over a flat, featureless landscape which many described as a 'billiard table'.

The Argentines, confident of their strength and evidently undeterred by the fall of their initial line of defence, unleashed a withering fire with mortars, artillery, heavy machine-guns, rifles and anti-aircraft guns, forcing C Company to ground. Without supporting fire over such a long distance, the advance stalled until mortar fire silenced the 20mm anti-aircraft gun on the western end of the airfield, but the crews declined to engage the artillery on the outskirts of Goose Green for fear of inflicting casualties on civilians. Still, clearly the defenders were determined to fight, bolstered as they were by the reinforcements helicoptered in from Stanley. Jenner called in fire support, only to be told by Keeble that none was to hand. Jenner, like Crosland during his struggle to take the Boca House position, strongly felt the absence of artillery support. C Company nonetheless persisted in the advance, although shells from the 105s near Goose Green wounded Jenner and killed or wounded eleven others in the process. Support Company now sought to engage the Argentines, albeit at extreme range from the forward slope of Darwin Hill. The Anti-Tank Platoon fired a missile at the two 35mm Oerlikon anti-aircraft guns on the peninsula, and though the wire reached its limit 75m short of the target, it frightened the crew off the position. While some platoons preserved their cover in the undulations of Darwin Ridge, others made a dash forward over the 400m of ground separating them from the schoolhouse, only to suffer several casualties and retire. Gains did occur elsewhere: by 1230 hrs two companies from C Company had reached the footbridge that allowed access across the estuary and along the track leading to Goose Green; yet with one para killed and eleven wounded in just a few minutes of assault, and still with 600m to cross to reach the airfield, a good deal remained to be done.

D Company, in the meantime, were forward of C Company, the former moving east and the latter moving south. A strong degree of confusion reigned, not least owing to D Company adopting a line of advance towards Goose Green that crossed C Company's objective, the airfield, so mixing personnel from both companies. D Company achieved progress by proceeding along a shallow valley, which offered cover from the anti-aircraft fire, and although exposed mines slowed Jenner's men, one of his platoons reached the outskirts of the airfield, there to encounter abandoned sangars. In short order it came under fire from the area around the flagpole, situated on a ridge just east of the airstrip, and withdrew. Elsewhere, while C and D Companies carried on towards their

A Sea King and Wessex resupply the troops at Goose Green. In theory troops could expect regular drops of ammunition, including mortar bombs. In reality, logistics over the fourteen hours of fighting left a great deal to be desired – but at no fault of the pilots and crews themselves. (Dr Stephen Hughes)

respective objectives, Crosland's B Company proceeded in its effort to swing east, enabling it to reach a position south of the airfield. In so doing, one of its platoons suppressed fire from the airfield and sent the anti-aircraft gunners scurrying for the protection of the settlement, leaving behind empty bunkers around the airfield and enabling B Company to approach from the south-west to within 400m of Goose Green itself as darkness began to descend.

We must now turn to the efforts to capture the schoolhouse and the fighting around the flagpole, which involved elements of both C and D Companies, some of whom, as related, became intermingled, causing confusion and rendering impossible any form of co-ordinated attack, now taking place twelve hours into the fighting. The school and the flagpole position offered points from which the Argentines could deny access from the north to Goose Green, their opponents' ultimate objective. C and D Companies were determined to capture them. A series of trenches and bunkers were situated around the flagpole, along which ran a track leading to Goose Green. In order to take it, Neame sought first to capture the school 300m away, so securing his flank before he could turn to attack the flagpole area. This area, however, was swept by small arms and artillery fire and became the site of the death of Capt. Barry, OC 12Pl D Company, who tried to arrange the surrender of troops holding the flagpole area. Accounts do not agree on the circumstances surrounding his death: some suggest he approached men signalling their intention to surrender, while others say he misinterpreted the situation and encountered 2nd Lt Centurion, who told him in clear English to return to his lines. Whatever the actual intention of the defenders, it seems clear that when someone fired a machine-gun, probably sited on Darwin Ridge, at long range, the Argentines opened fire at their closest target, killing Barry at point blank range.

At the same time, elements of both C and D Companies were tasked with attacking the school, though neither attempted any form of co-ordination and the whole affair became a confused effort. The details of this are not clear, since sub-units became

HANDLING THE DEAD

The day after the battle, a Wessex brought most of the British dead to Ajax Bay for medical inspection and burial.
Dr Rick Jolly noted in his diary the procedure he followed:
'The cold wet clothing is deftly cut away. The pockets examined, and personal possessions sorted, logged and put in a plastic bag. In several cases the spare Victory berets which all the Paras seem to carry are so badly soaked in blood as to be unfit for return to the relatives. With the corpse stripped naked in the freezing air, under a clear blue sky, I then carefully examine each body to certify both death and its cause.' He then filled out the requisite field death certificates and ordered the bodies returned to their plastic bags. Most families had their loved ones repatriated to the UK.

intermingled, as noted, in a contest that began around 1300 hrs and occurred simultaneously with the challenge for possession of the airfield. The assault on the school began when paras proceeded from the western end of the estuary and rapidly reached an area housing a dairy and outbuildings, as well as the school itself – all positions defended by troops in nearby trenches. As at Boca House and along Darwin Ridge, fighting involved the now indispensable 66mm rocket, as well as grenades and SLRs. The school soon caught fire and the survivors from within fled south in the direction of the settlement. The defenders answered with anti-aircraft guns situated on the Goose Green peninsula, hitting the blazing school building with accurate fire but failing to impede the paras' advance. After more confused fighting near the school and at the airfield, by around 1500 hrs the fighting amidst these positions slackened and finally subsided as the Argentines withdrew into the settlement. Keeble instructed Neame not to advance further, but to assume a defensive position.

At about the same time, two Aeromacchi jets appeared over the isthmus and strafed D Company with cannon fire, dispersing the men but inflicting no damage as they dived for cover. One aircraft was downed by a Blowpipe fired by Support Company and the other disappeared from view, giving the briefest of respites from air attack. Then, a few minutes later at about 1515 hrs, two Pucaras approached from the north-west and dropped napalm canisters, narrowly missing a D Company platoon position, though causing consternation as the intense heat momentarily drew away the troops' oxygen and warmed their faces and hands. A hail of small arms fire brought down one of the Pucaras, leaving some of Crosland's men doused in aviation fuel as the plane descended and the pilot ejected, gliding into captivity. The other Pucara managed to reach Stanley, albeit heavily damaged. The hitherto absence of British aircraft was the consequence of poor visibility at sea; that now changed, so that the paras had hardly seen off the Pucaras and Aeromacchis when around 1530 hrs three Harriers roared overhead, long awaited by 2 Para as a decisive means with which to neutralise the two 35mm Oerlikons on the peninsula east of Goose Green. As these were close to the settlement, the pilots had to take extreme care to avoid civilian casualties; possibly as a result, both Harriers missed, dropping their cluster bombs into the sea, but causing an impressive spectacle as the water reacted violently to the detonations. The third Harrier managed to hit some Argentines on the peninsula, although crucially not the guns, which continued to fire.

The Last Act

	1600 hrs	Situation at dusk: A Company on Darwin Hill; B Company digging in on high ground 2km (1.2 miles) south-west of Goose Green; C Company just west of settlement; D Company east of airfield close to settlement
28 May	1630 hrs	Combat Team Solari arrives 5 or 6km (3 or 4 miles) south of Goose Green
	1900 hrs	Combat Team commander sends a patrol into Goose Green settlement to assess the situation
	2245 hrs	Argentine patrol reports that Task Force Mercedes is surrounded
	2330 hrs	Combat Team Solari enters settlement
29 May	0930 hrs	Senior officers from both sides meet to discuss Argentine terms of surrender
	1000 hrs	Air Commodore Pedroza and Lt Col Piaggi surrender to Maj. Keeble

At about 1600 hrs, as the light began to fade, it was by no means clear to 2 Para that the battle was over. A Company stood on Darwin Hill and occupied that position through the night; B Company had succeeded in executing its wide movement south of the airfield and now stood about 2km (1.2 miles) south-west of Goose Green, from where the Argentines continued to fire until darkness set in. Worse still, as night descended eight Argentine helicopters offloaded reinforcements of approximately 100 men under Capt.

Eduardo Corsiglia to the south-west of B Company's position. Crosland was worried: D Company were far off – in fact 2,000m away – and his company was short of ammunition and severely fatigued after almost sixteen hours of uninterrupted fighting. He therefore sensibly ordered his men to withdraw to higher ground and dig in, thus seeking protection from possible counter-attack. They carried on with their work until 0200 hrs: exhausted, hungry and huddled together against intense cold and the first signs of snowfall. C Company, meanwhile, withdrew to the gorse gully

A Regimental Medical Officer (RMO) from 2 Para treats Argentine casualties at the RAP at Camilla Creek. (Dr Stephen Hughes)

to regroup after the attack on the school had succeeded, but the impetus of Jenner's assault had run its course and, in any event, the Argentines had retreated into the comparative safety of the settlement as darkness approached. Neame's D Company had orders to regroup and not to advance any further that night. All the paras thus spent the freezing night completely worn out, hungry, short of water and gravely low on ammunition. This constituted their third night with practically no sleep, a minimal amount of food and a great physical and psychological toll exacted on them since before they had even reached Camilla Creek House. Some still had plenty of work to do: the wounded not yet evacuated were to be removed by Land Rover and helicopter, and men from all companies went out in search of the unrecovered wounded.

The situation was, therefore, mixed: the battalion had driven the Argentines from their positions, but had not yet taken Darwin and Goose Green. The men were desperate for rest and resupply, and had lost sixteen dead and thirty-one wounded. The Argentines had been reinforced by a company, which reached Goose Green in the dark but whose presence was probably not sufficient to embolden Piaggi

The Community Centre at Goose Green, into which the Argentines concentrated all the residents on the isthmus. No civilians were injured or killed in the fighting, but in his summons to the Argentine commander Major Keeble reserved the right to bombard the settlement in accordance with the laws of war. (Dr Stephen Hughes)

to renew the fighting the following morning. In short, with his men scattered across the isthmus and exhausted, Keeble could not be certain that the gains of 28 May would go unchallenged on the 29th.

He appreciated, however, that Argentine spirits must be low – perhaps close to breaking point – and therefore decided to encourage their surrender. He received a promise from Brig. Thompson for reinforcements and additional firepower, the combination of which Keeble planned, if necessary, to employ in the form of a demonstration of force to overawe the defenders, imbue in them a sense of the futility of further resistance, and thereby force a capitulation. Barring that, Keeble received authorisation to bombard Goose Green, follow up with an assault and finish the job the hard way – though he certainly did not wish to exercise the latter option, particularly in light of the civilian casualties inevitably to be caused. Before dawn, a radio message was sent to the Argentines in Goose Green that a party bearing a flag of truce would approach their position around first light. Two prisoners were duly sent forward to present the terms, written in Spanish, with stress placed on the issue of the civilians' safety, which Piaggi was reminded, barring the residents' release from captivity, remained his responsibility under the rules of war. To Keeble's considerable relief, Argentine commanders agreed to assemble near the airfield to discuss the terms of surrender. The fact was that, despite being reinforced, Piaggi found himself surrounded and could not possibly put up a successful defence on the 29th. Consequently, at 0930 hrs a meeting took place between senior officers from both sides. As a result, the British delegation persuaded their counterparts that, having fought well, they could lay down their arms with honour. Keen to encourage this impression amongst the vanquished, Keeble permitted them to conduct a ceremony, complete with a speech and a chorus of their national anthem, before more than 1,000 personnel grounded arms in a field near the church.

The Battle of Goose Green was over at a cost of sixteen dead to 2 Para, including its commanding officer, plus a Royal Marine and a Royal Engineer, both on detached duty from their

Argentine prisoners and paras after the fighting at Goose Green. The former were repatriated almost immediately after the war ended, but officers were held longer as a guarantee that their government fully complied with the surrender terms encompassing the whole of the Falklands, and South Thule, in the South Sandwich Islands.

respective units. The Argentines lost fifty-five killed and several times that number wounded.

The strategic significance of Goose Green will be analysed later; but the immediate results were readily apparent to Pte Tony Banks of D Company, who in his memoirs recalled:

> Slowly, locals started to emerge from the church and village hall. They were so grateful for us being there. We were heroes to them and we felt like liberators ... When we saw them, and discovered that they were just like us Brits, not like Argies at all, we thought, yes, this is right – what we've done here.
>
> (Banks, *Storming the Falklands*, p. 133.)

AFTER THE BATTLE:
STRATEGIC POSTSCRIPT

Preparations for the Advance on Stanley

The Battle of Goose Green represented only the beginning of the British ground offensive. On 27 May, as 2 Para left Sussex Mountain for Camilla Creek House prior to battle, Thompson's advance east got underway in the form of two epic treks to Mount Kent. These involved 45 Commando's 'yomp' (the Royal Marines' expression for a loaded march, an abbreviation for 'your own marching pace') and 3 Para's 'tab' (army-speak for 'tactical advance to battle'), both conducted on foot by virtue of the loss of helicopters aboard the *Atlantic Conveyor*. The first leg of 45 Commando's march took them to Teal Inlet, 40km (25 miles) from the beachhead at San Carlos, leaving another 32km (20 miles) to the nearest Argentine positions, which dotted the elevated points west of Stanley. These consisted of Mount Harriet, Two Sisters and Mount Longdon in the first line of defence, and Mount Tumbledown, Wireless Ridge and Mount William in the second. As weather conditions grew worse daily, Thompson understood the advance represented a race against the clock.

The two units traversed broken ground with Bergens often exceeding 50kg (110lb) in weight, in what would become a stunning example of determination and remarkable endurance

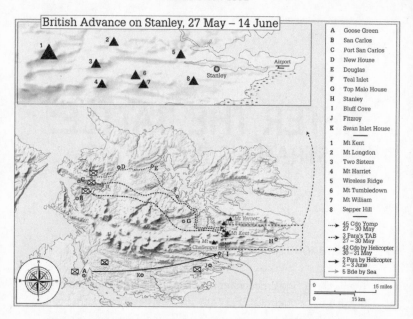

British Advance on Stanley, 27 May – 14 June

A	Goose Green
B	San Carlos
C	Port San Carlos
D	New House
E	Douglas
F	Teal Inlet
G	Top Malo House
H	Stanley
I	Bluff Cove
J	Fitzroy
K	Swan Inlet House
1	Mt Kent
2	Mt Longdon
3	Two Sisters
4	Mt Harriet
5	Wireless Ridge
6	Mt Tumbledown
7	Mt William
8	Sapper Hill

····▶ 45 Cdo Yomp
27 – 30 May
··▶ 3 Para's TAB
27 – 30 May
··▶ 42 Cdo by Helicopter
30 – 31 May
──▶ 2 Para by Helicopter
2 – 3 June
──▶ 5 Bde by Sea

0   15 miles

0   15 km

that was to take the marines first to Douglas Settlement and then on to Teal Inlet, which they reached on the night of 30 May. 3 Para, meanwhile, had a shorter distance to cover to Teal, which they accomplished without the benefit of marked tracks: a 53km (33-mile) slog, which required them to bed down without even the benefit of sleeping bags, entering the tiny settlement on the night of 28 May. Both units then proceeded to Mount Estancia and Mount Vernet, the unopposed occupation of which gave them control of a chain of peaks 11km (7 miles) long, leaving the Argentines defending half a dozen key points a few miles to the east. With helicopters freed from transporting such considerable numbers of paras and marines, they were available to convey guns to within range of Argentine forces as close as the outskirts of Stanley – many at Wireless Ridge and a handful on Sapper Hill. Nevertheless, with 3 Commando Brigade's supply line now fully stretched, 45 Commando and 3 Para could for the moment move no further. Their achievement fully confirmed their reputation for extreme

DIFFICULT, EXPOSED GROUND

The terrain at Goose Green was largely boggy and, of what solid ground existed, the troops found it covered in 'babies' heads', the name given to describe the round tussocks of grass ubiquitous to the islands. Owing to the unevenness and hardness of the 'babies heads', a soldier could easily twist an ankle or knee, particularly in the dark, thus rendering him *hors de combat* even before he made contact with the enemy.

fitness and unfaltering determination. On 30–31 May, helicopters transported 42 Commando forward to Mount Kent, just on the eve of the first snowfall. Teal Inlet became the new forward supply base, with vitally required rations and ammunition brought by sea from San Carlos. Three battalions now stood poised to engage the first line of Argentine defence – all accomplished within a week of Thompson's orders to advance.

On 30 May, Major General (Maj. Gen.) Jeremy Moore and Brig. Tony Wilson arrived at San Carlos, with Moore assuming from Thompson the position of Land Forces Commander Falkland Islands, while Wilson waited for the arrival of his 5 Brigade, consisting of a battalion each of the Royal Gurkha Rifles, the Welsh Guards and the Scots Guards, plus supporting arms from the Royal Artillery, Royal Engineers, Royal Signals, Royal Electrical and Mechanical Engineers, the Royal Army Medical Corps and other corps. Thompson moved the headquarters of 3 Commando Brigade to Teal Inlet, enabling him to control his forces at closer proximity to their new positions, while Moore found the circumstances of his new command looking very positive: he controlled a secure base at San Carlos, a fully functioning forward operating base at Teal Inlet, and 2 Para had achieved a resounding victory at Goose Green.

When 5 Brigade arrived at San Carlos, most of it was earmarked for movement east on the southern flank facing the Stanley defences, though a continued shortage of helicopters prevented

Moore from shifting most of 5 Brigade east while at the same time trying to provide the food and ammunition needed for the forward units from 3 Commando Brigade. The Gurkhas, however, were put to good use replacing 2 Para at Goose Green. Wilson wanted to move his brigade on foot to the mountains west of Stanley via the southern route. However, in the absence of settlements in which his troops could rest and resupply on the route to Fitzroy, a distance of 56km (35 miles) from Goose Green, and in light of the fact that neither of the two guards battalions, in contrast to the paras and marines, were accustomed to marching such distances, the 5 Brigade commander had to abandon this plan. Nevertheless, when a small group from 2 Para, travelling by helicopter, discovered Fitzroy and Bluff Cove free of Argentine troops, Moore ordered the whole battalion shifted by Chinook and Scout helicopters, which they accomplished on 2–3 June, with most of 5 Brigade to follow by sea since helicopters were needed to ferry supplies forward. Accordingly, the Scots Guards arrived safely at Bluff Cove on 6 June. The Welsh Guards followed in their wake, only to come under air attack near Fitzroy while aboard the *Sir Galahad* on the morning of 8 June, losing fifty-four dead and about 150 wounded in a fiery inferno, which left most of the battalion *hors de combat* for the remainder of the fighting.

The campaign now reached its climax, consisting of a series of engagements fought in the mountains just west of Stanley. Even without the troops lost at Goose Green, Menendez still commanded more than 11,000 troops across the islands. Moreover, even after deducting those garrisoning West Falkland, where they could perform no useful purpose in halting the British advance, this still left about 9,000 men in and around Stanley, although only about 5,500 of whom consisted of infantry, with those in the mountains much demoralised by cold, the shortage of food and knowledge of the defeat of their comrades at Goose Green. With such troops – a combination of stalwart marines and infantry of mixed levels of motivation and experience – Menendez could not hope to halt the forward progress of British forces and now faced the prospect of

A British helicopter ferrying equipment via underslung netting. Both sides suffered badly from insufficient numbers of helicopters. Across a landscape almost totally lacking in roads, this left the attackers short of equipment and ammunition and obliged many of their troops to 'yomp' or 'tab', while the same problem denied the Argentines the ability to launch a counter-attack against the beachhead at San Carlos.

imminent defeat. True, his forces occupied sangars, bunkers and trenches covered by machine-guns and artillery, and in many cases protected with extensive minefields; but the Argentines had failed to establish defences in depth, with sufficient numbers or enjoying a proper degree of fire support.

Moore had originally planned to attack the defences around Stanley on the evening of 8–9 June, but shortages of supplies – in particular the lack of sufficient artillery shells close to the frontline – delayed this by two nights. A further postponement of twenty-four hours occurred when the crippling of the *Sir Galahad* interfered with the helicopter schedules, although other helicopters arrived via another vessel on 9 June. These circumstances thus delayed the movement of British troops in forward areas by four days and nights in adverse conditions – specifically, 3 Para, 45 Commando and 42 Commando, all situated in the areas around Mounts Vernet, Kent and Challenger, with the Scots

Guards from 5 Brigade beyond Bluff Cove. The British had to attack imminently before increasingly harsh conditions – especially rapidly dropping temperatures in exposed positions – sapped their strength, damaged their health and consequently affected operational effectiveness. Exposure had yet to take a significant toll, but this was now only a matter of time. Further delays could also compromise success, particularly when heavy seas threatened to imperil marine supply lines. The Argentines were scarcely better off in terms of the effects of deteriorating weather, but their conditions stood marginally better, with shelter established in prepared positions and in Stanley behind them, whereas British troops now stood well east of San Carlos.

All the while, logistical support continued with remarkable efficiency, and without which the ground forces simply could not operate. Troops poised for an attack on the Stanley defences depended upon a supply chain which extended not simply to Teal Inlet, Fitzroy or San Carlos, but stretched on to Ascension Island and all the way back to Britain. This whole chain depended upon thousands, including: helicopter crews; personnel of the Royal Logistic Corps tasked with moving supplies to forward areas; the crews of the supply ships; the crews of the Hercules transports flying sixteen-hour long-haul flights to and from Ascension carrying supplies; the tanker crews at Ascension; and the transport squadrons of the RAF, which flew regular missions from bases at Lyneham and Brize Norton with essential supplies from Britain. This extraordinary capability highlights the degree to which Britain had by this time achieved naval supremacy and air superiority and could maintain a secure air bridge at least as far as Ascension – almost exactly midway to the Falklands – while Argentine forces only 650km from the mainland suffered from shortages in food and artillery shells. British forces on the outskirts of Stanley, on the other hand, found themselves adequately supplied, albeit with problems associated with the climate.

Moore shifted his headquarters from San Carlos to Fitzroy and laid plans for the coming offensive – the largest of its kind since the Second World War. For this task he had available the equivalent of seven battalions of infantry: 42 and 45 Commando, 2 and 3 Para, 1st Welsh Guards, 2nd Scots Guards and 1/7th Gurkhas (minus one company detached at Goose Green). In support, the artillery supplied thirty 105mm guns. There was also limited armoured support in the form of eight light tanks of the Blues and Royals, but the rough and steep terrain was understood to render them of limited use against some of the elevated Argentine positions. Moore had two strategic options: attacking on a broad front or on a narrow one. A narrow thrust through the south, which would avoid confrontation with the Argentine positions in the north, would necessitate the capture of Mount Harriet and Two Sisters by one brigade, followed by Mount Tumbledown and Mount William by the other. This would then leave only the less formidable obstacle of Sapper Hill before Stanley itself. This plan would obviate the need to engage the Argentines in potentially expensive operations against Mount Longdon and Wireless Ridge. Moreover, the plan suited the circumstances of limited supply of artillery ammunition, with shells required only against a few objectives instead of a broad range. However, after careful thought, the plan proved unworkable: the attacks would be impossible without artillery support and the guns would have to be moved by helicopter from behind Mount Kent to the large, exposed area of ground in front of this feature before the second phase of the attack could proceed. In order to transport the guns and all the other supplies and equipment required for that phase, the helicopters would be obliged to follow the route past the north end of Mount Kent – a position covered by Mount Longdon, which the Argentines controlled. This thus left Moore with no option but to proceed on a broad front.

Having established the objectives, Moore worked out a plan for attacks to be conducted over two successive nights, beginning on 11–12 June. 3 Commando Brigade would move first: against Mount Longdon, Two Sisters and Mount Harriet on the first night, followed on the second by both brigades engaged against Tumbledown, Mount William and Wireless Ridge. Success might induce the Argentines to surrender but, if not, Moore planned to push ahead against Sapper Hill on the third night, thus denying the garrison in Stanley all positions of prominence to the west of the town. By attacking at night, Moore could take advantage of his troops' superior fighting capability and mitigate some of the disadvantages of moving across ground completely exposed to the fire of entrenched defenders armed with rifles, machine-guns, mortars and grenades.

It will be recalled that the Task Force had been rushed to the South Atlantic in order, first, to avoid the problems arising out of the UN calling for a ceasefire and subsequent talks; and second, to engage the Argentines before the full onset of winter put a halt to operations and enabled the garrison to remain as a *fait accompli*. Now, with temperatures steadily dropping, practically all Moore's forces committed to the fight and his supply lines were vulnerable, and everything depended on a very narrow timetable – a fortnight at the outside – in which to defeat the Argentines and re-establish control over the islands.

For the attacks planned for 11–12 June against Mount Harriet, Mount Longdon and Two Sisters, Thompson decided on a night assault – a sensible decision based on a number of considerations. He knew the Argentines controlled all the prominent positions covering the western approaches to Stanley and appreciated that each could provide mutual support to the others, often with flanking fire. The ground over which his forces had to move was invariably open, highly exposed and easy to defend. It was impossible to be certain of the level of resistance that would be encountered, but regular units of the Argentine army were known to be in the area and even if some of the conscripts could not withstand a determined attack, Thompson had to be careful not to assume victory would come as quickly as it had at Goose Green. He therefore regarded it as vital to capture the three principal mountains – Longdon, Harriet and Two Sisters – in a single co-ordinated brigade attack. He possessed the necessary highly trained, elite units units to do so: 2 and 3 Para, and 42 and 45 Commando, all trained in night fighting and highly motivated.

Operations on 11–12 June: Mount Harriet, Mount Longdon and Two Sisters

On 11–12 June, 42 Commando was responsible for seizing Mount Harriet, a position held by the 4th Infantry Regiment. Patrols provided first-rate intelligence, including the whereabouts of some of the minefields laid by the defenders, but their commander, Lt Col Nick Vaux, had no aerial reconnaissance photographs to assist him and without these he had to rely on information about the ground, and the strength and disposition of the defenders, exclusively from material brought back by RM and Special Forces patrols. Mount Harriet dominated the ground over the track connecting Goose Green and Stanley, which the Argentines had used heavily for resupply. The area was also heavily mined, particularly on the western and southern slopes – the directions from which the Argentines expected to resist an attack. Vaux's plan involved a long march south of Harriet along its right flank in order to seize the position from the rear, capitalising on intelligence collected by a patrol, which had discovered a route unencumbered by mines. Since the Argentines were very likely to have established particularly strong positions at both ends of the mountain, 42 Commando was to assault from the south-east by advancing over an extended distance, avoiding the minefields, crossing two tracks and skirting a lake. Success depended on approaching in silence and in darkness. Unlike the attacks carried out the same night against Mount Longdon and Two Sisters, Vaux planned to dispense with the element of surprise by employing a noisy pre-assault deception plan involving machine-gun and artillery fire directed from the west, leaving the impression that this was to constitute the direction of the main assault.

Two Sisters, which 45 Commando Royal Marines captured in darkness on 11–12 June in the wake of their 'yomp' across the island – an extraordinary feat of endurance which only elite forces could achieve. (Author)

The leading company crossed the start line at 2200 hrs and soon encountered resistance from small arms and artillery, but despite this heavy fire Vaux's plan succeeded: the Argentines did not anticipate an attack from the rear, though they offered vigorous resistance nonetheless. As at Goose Green, the 66mm light anti-tank weapon proved its versatility in destroying Argentine positions among the rocks, allowing the momentum of attack to continue uninterrupted over the course of the eight hours of fighting, which saw 42 Commando drive the Argentines off Mount Harriet so successfully that no counter-attack took place. The marines lost two killed and seventeen wounded. The Argentines lost about twenty-five killed plus a staggering 300 prisoners. Vaux's strategy had succeeded brilliantly; made possible only by troops possessing a high state of fitness, by virtue of exemplary training in manoeuvring and by exercising an impressive capacity for fighting at night over rugged terrain.

The plan underpinning the attack on Mount Longdon, on 3 Commando Brigade's northern flank, followed the pattern devised for Harriet and Two Sisters: with little natural cover available to his troops and a large distance to traverse, Thompson appreciated that he risked suffering heavy casualties from areas swept by small arms and artillery fire. As with the other objectives of 11–12 June, he opted for a night attack, which would provide ten hours for his troops to reach their objectives. Full use of the time available was necessary given the inherent difficulties of moving and fighting over broken ground, which always slowed the advance and usually increased the casualty rate. He therefore determined that 3 Para's attack should be conducted in silence and without supporting artillery fire, thus preserving, if possible, the element of surprise. Any opponents unfamiliar with fighting at night would be bewildered and less effective, and this was thus to the attackers' advantage. From approximately 2015 hrs the moonlit night would provide at least a silhouette of the elevated ground, so offering a modicum of direction as the paras advanced. Moreover, the attack would be aided by guns of the Royal Artillery, who had 11,000 shells at their disposal, as well as with naval gunfire support, consisting of up to 1,400 rounds to be directed by forward observers. Harriers could supply close air support as soon as dawn emerged.

With a week to collect information, those planning the assault on Mount Longdon acquired a fairly clear understanding of the ground

The west face of Mount Longdon, the approach taken during 3 Para's attack on 11–12 June. Longdon is a long ridge running east to west, with open ground leading up to it from all directions for 915m (1,000yd), making it a formidable defensive position. Fighting here inflicted the heaviest toll on British ground forces in a single day.

to be covered and the forces opposing them. This rocky eminence consisted of a long ridge running east to west, with open ground leading up to it from all directions for over 1,000yd. Minefields, discovered by patrols, lay on the southern flank and reports indicated that the Argentines were well dug in on Wireless Ridge, about 1,000yd to the east. 3 Para's CO, Lt Col Hugh Pike, had effectively no option but to attack west to east, so avoiding accidental contact with 45 Commando to his right and probably enabling him to isolate the defenders on the western end of the ridge from any potential support from the eastern end. The paras proceeded just after sunset, around 1600 hrs, giving them four hours of movement before the moon rose, and thus providing some cover of darkness during the approach to their start line. Pike devised a simple plan of attack: two companies forward to be pitted against well-trained and disciplined marines, and most of the 7th Infantry Regiment. Some of the Argentines were equipped with night sights with sufficient intensity to provide a near-daylight view. This advantage, combined with the open ground extending over half a mile from the base of Longdon, offered the defenders an exceptionally good position and presented no option to 3 Para but to cross this expanse before ascending slopes that rose several hundred feet.

The attack got underway at 2015 hrs, with the approach proceeding well as the paras moved quietly up the slope. The light of the moon soon illuminated the summit and the heights before them, with silence reigning until a para stepped on a mine, so alerting the defenders, who quickly responded with artillery fire. Although many Argentines were caught completely by surprise, at this point artillery and heavy machine-guns forced the foremost attackers to ground. Nevertheless, the Argentines could not hold back the advance, supported as it was by the heavy weight of fire put down by mortars, artillery and machine-guns, which enabled the paras to clear defenders from their trenches and sangars with rifles, bayonets and grenades, taking prisoners as they advanced. In what amounted in all to eight hours of difficult and costly fighting conducted entirely in darkness, the Argentines put up a

Goose Green settlement today – largely unchanged after more than three decades. No fighting took place here – the schoolhouse stood slightly to the north – and thus all its residents emerged unscathed. (Author)

respectable defence and inflicted a toll of seventeen killed and forty wounded on 3 Para, but at a cost of fifty defenders killed and about the same number taken captive.

In the centre of the eminences immediately west of Stanley stood Two Sisters, the third British objective for the night of 11–12 June. This feature consisted of two peaks each of about 1,000ft in elevation, extending over 1 mile in length from west to east and notable for its five jagged ridges, which formed a ragged spine. A company of conscripts from the 4th Regiment, which had established a strong defensive position including heavy machine-guns and mortars, held this formidable position. Responsibility for its capture fell to 45 Commando, who had already shown some of their formidable mettle during their yomp from San Carlos.

Their commanding officer, Colonel (Col) Andrew Whitehead, laid plans involving an attack in two phases. While the marines would approach in silence, support was available if necessary from the guns of HMS *Glamorgan* and *Yarmouth*, artillery and the 81mm mortars attached to 45 Commando itself. The attack began at 2300 hrs,

Looking towards Two Sisters and Goat Ridge from Mount Longdon. Two Sisters, which lay approximately 1,500m south-west of Longdon, witnessed a brilliantly executed, simultaneous action (with 42 Commando on Harriet and 3 Para on Longdon) conducted by 45 Commando Royal Marines.

to be met by bursts of heavy machine-gun fire, which obliged the leading company to temporarily withdraw from one of the features. With Milans and mortar fire, some marines managed to reach the summit, only to be thrown back by artillery fire before again pushing on, finally to overwhelm the machine-gun positions and secure part of the position. Elsewhere on this rocky feature, the defenders sent up a flare to illuminate the sky and, observing the direction of attack, offered a stormy response. This was highlighted by heavy artillery and mortars, which characterised the stiff resistance met by 45 Commando who, only after deploying anti-tank weapons and further hard fighting with their SLRs, finally prevailed and secured possession of Two Sisters by dawn. The fall of Two Sisters represented a serious blow to the Argentine main defences, yet the marines only lost three killed and one sapper from the Royal Engineers – all from artillery or mortar fire. 45 Commando took forty-four prisoners and killed about ten of the defenders. The remaining Argentines fled eastwards, probably into Stanley. The marines had received excellent support from the Royal Artillery, who had fired about 1,500 rounds – precisely the sort of firepower 2 Para had needed at Goose Green.

Mount Tumbledown, which fell on the night of 11–12 June to the Scots Guards after close-quarter fighting involving the bayonet – a rare phenomenon in late twentieth-century combat. (Author)

The three engagements fought on the briskly cold night of 11–12 June may be seen collectively as a remarkable success for the British, who had defeated a numerically superior force in its main defensive positions. However, the fighting had been more prolonged than expected, rendering impossible further exploitation eastwards. All told, the British suffered twenty-four fatal casualties and approximately sixty-five wounded, with a disproportionate share falling on 3 Para, with nineteen dead from the difficult frontal assault against Mount Longdon, juxtaposed with the Royal Marines' two assaults involving flanking approaches which resulted in only five men dead.

Operations on 12–13 June: Mount Tumbledown and Wireless Ridge

On the evening of 12–13 June the offensive resumed, with the main effort to come from 5 Brigade in the south against the Stanley defences, involving an attack by the Second Battalion the Scots Guards against Tumbledown and further north, an assault by 2 Para against Wireless Ridge. The Royal Artillery would furnish five batteries of guns to support these efforts, together with four warships and the eight tanks of the Blues and Royals, which had proceeded across the island from San Carlos. Mount Tumbledown

131

constituted a very formidable position held by elements of the 5th Marine Battalion – perhaps the best sizeable unit the Argentines possessed on the islands – and represented the key post in the defences west of Stanley. In the assessment of Lt Col Scott, the battalion's commander, an attack across the exposed southern slopes of the mountain posed too great a risk to his guardsmen, so he instead chose a western advance along the summit ridge without the benefit of supporting fire, thereby ensuring as quiet an approach as possible. In the first phase, a diversionary raid carried out along the Fitzroy–Stanley track would precede the seizure by one company of the western end of the eminence, while in the second phase another company was to capture the area around the summit. Lastly, a third company would seize the eastern end.

The diversion began at 2030 hrs, with the main advance commencing half an hour later amidst freezing conditions. Supported by light tanks, the diversionary force engaged the Argentines for two hours, followed by limited success by other sub-units employing anti-armour weapons against Argentine bunkers; indeed, despite the efforts of guardsman to use grenades at perilously close range, they still found their progress severely held up. Around 0230 hrs the attackers called in artillery support in order to break the impasse, and after several instances of hand-to-hand combat a handful of men finally reached the summit – but only after a seven-hour fight, complete with bayonets bloodied. Other companies made extensive use of their 84mm Carl Gustav anti-armour weapons and light anti-tank weapons. Fighting did not cease until about 0815 hrs on 13 June, long after sunrise, in the course of which the Scots Guards suffered nine killed: two during the diversion and five in the main assault, plus a further two from mortar fire when shells landed while the men tended the wounded. It took just over eleven hours from the moment they left their start line for the guardsmen to wrest the ridge from the Argentines, of whom twelve were made prisoner and perhaps three times that number killed. It represented a significant achievement, though it took much longer than had been envisioned, a circumstance almost certainly attributable to the fact that the best Argentine units were deployed there. With the fall of Tumbledown went the key feature in the defence of Stanley. The Argentines evacuated their troops from Mount William that night, leaving only Wireless Ridge as the last elevated position to stand in the path of the British offensive.

Buoyed up by their victory at Goose Green and the only major unit to be given a second crack at the Argentines, 2 Para were assigned the task of seizing Wireless Ridge on the same night as the Scots Guards' attack on Tumbledown, 12–13 June. Standing 3.2km (2 miles) to the north-east of Tumbledown, Wireless Ridge constituted in fact two separate pieces of high ground, which Lt Col David Chaundler decided to attack from the north. Whereas 2 Para had received very little fire support at Goose Green, quite the reverse was planned for the attack against Wireless Ridge. Here, the battalion possessed many mortars of their own as well as some from 3 Para, two batteries of artillery placed at their disposal through the course of the night, other guns provided by the Royal Artillery if needed, and the firepower of HMS *Ambuscade*. Finally, two Scorpions and two Scimitars from the Blues and Royals were available, capable of offering close support since the ground here – in contrast to the other features assaulted thus far – offered no steep sides. The defending 7th Regiment, which had fought 3 Para on Mount Longdon, deployed the usual rifle companies, plus snipers, heavy machine-guns, mortars and artillery.

Chaundler divided his plan into four phases to include preparatory artillery fire. The leading company left its start line at 2145 hrs, supported by the Scimitars and Scorpions, and on reaching one of the heights discovered the defenders had withdrawn under the weight of incoming fire. Yet, while the paras sought to consolidate this newly occupied ground, they themselves became the target of an artillery barrage. At this point, to the east, two other companies began their advance from the start line and prepared to engage the defenders when

> ## KEEBLE'S PLAN TO SECURE ARGENTINE SURRENDER AT GOOSE GREEN
>
> Although after the Harrier attack in the afternoon Keeble believed the Argentines' will to carry on was beginning to crack, he appreciated that his own acute shortage of ammunition would not allow him to prosecute the attack further. He therefore developed two plans, the first to demonstrate a sense of his complete mastery of the situation, albeit constituting something of a bluff: 'I remember sitting in a gorse bush behind Darwin Hill that night and saying to Dair Farrar-Hockley, commanding A Company, and others that the way to crack the problem was to walk down the hill the next day and tell the bloody Argies the game was up and defeat inevitable.' (Arthur, *Above All, Courage*, p. 192)

the Argentines, bowing to the pressure of the combination of artillery, mortar and machine-gun fire directed against their position, withdrew. Meanwhile, another company of paras, supported by the light tanks of the Blues and Royals together with Milans and machine-guns, made steady progress. Indeed, 2 Para succeeded in seizing the first half of the ridge with little effort, but the defenders offered stubborn resistance over the remaining half, with the attackers obliged to clear one bunker after the next. Their advance never faltered, however, and eventually the defence collapsed, leaving Chaundler's battalion in possession of the ridge. At daybreak a small force of Argentines assaulted the position, only to be repulsed by the defenders and supporting fire drawn from mortars and 105mm guns. As the sun rose higher the Argentines fled in the direction of Stanley.

Unlike at Goose Green, at Wireless Ridge 2 Para had encountered little resistance, received significant fire support from tanks and artillery and had learned from the hard experience of a fortnight before. The fall of Wireless Ridge and Mount Tumbledown broke the back of the Argentine defensive network near Stanley and

B Company 2 Para after its entry into Stanley, where they found the roads littered with rubbish and the contents of houses looted by occupying forces. A yawning gap existed between the discipline exercised by the two combatants, reflecting the very different approaches British and Argentine platoon and company commanders took towards the men under their command.

on 14 June, in defiance of Galtieri's orders to hold out, Menendez agreed to a ceasefire, his outright surrender becoming effective at 2059 hrs local time.

The war was over, but at a cost: British service personnel suffered 252 fatal casualties across all services engaged – Army, Royal Marines, Royal Navy, Royal Air Force, the Royal Fleet Auxiliary and the Merchant Navy. Three Falkland Islanders were also killed. Of this total, the Royal Marines lost twenty-six killed and the Army 148 personnel. The Task Force as a whole lost four warships and a landing craft, one fleet auxiliary and one merchantman. Helicopter losses amounted to twenty-three from the Royal Navy, seven from the Royal Air Force, three from the Royal Marines and one from the Army. Argentine fatalities amounted to about 750, of whom 261 served in the army and thirty-seven in the marines. In addition, approximately 1,100 personnel were wounded or fell ill. Well-documented figures for Argentine prisoners reveal that 12,978 personnel fell into British hands during the whole spectrum of operations, from the re-capture of South Georgia to the surrender of South Thule in the South Sandwich Islands.

THE LEGACY:
LESSONS LEARNED
FROM GOOSE GREEN

A number of key factors may be identified as having contributed to the belligerents' success or failure on the ground, thus revealing some important 'lessons learned' to be derived from an analysis of the engagement. In light of the very closely matched numbers involved and the type and availability of support weapons available to both sides, there is no question that victory or defeat hinged not on weapons or numbers, but on knowledge and use of the ground, professionalism, training, leadership, and the relative strength of each side's fighting spirit. In all of these factors, the British demonstrated a marked superiority. These, and other elements, help explain the otherwise unlikely outcome of the Battle of Goose Green.

Professionalism and *Esprit de Corps*

There can be little doubt about the yawning gulf that existed between the level of training and motivation characterising Argentine and British forces. The paras were professional soldiers, trained to the very highest standards and possessed of a fighting spirit second to none within the British Army – and probably a match for any other elite, regular fighting force of equal strength anywhere

The memorial to the fallen at Goose Green, erected within days of their liberation by local residents, who fashioned the black steel cross from scrap metal and mounted it on a stone cairn cemented together. It stands in a position seen from both Darwin and Goose Green.

in the world. By contrast, only the Argentine officers and NCOs present at Goose Green were professionals; the rank and file consisted of a combination of raw recruits with a few months' training or reservists who had completed a year's service – but no more.

Esprit de corps figured as a prominent component of professionalism, and in this respect, the cobbled-together, composite units under Piaggi's command offered nothing comparable to the strong sense of regimental integrity and close-knit bond characteristic of their airborne-trained opponents. Nowhere was that spirit more strongly embodied than in the person of Lt Col Jones who, however one judges his temperament, epitomised the inspirational leadership long associated with para officers, junior and senior alike. Chris Keeble rightly observed that success rested on his shoulders:

> The victory … was H's. The inspiration of 2 Para came from him, and my role was merely to act on his behalf in his absence. For that I am the caretaker of an enamelled bit of metal, which I carry on behalf of every man in 2 Para, especially the junior non-commissioned officers and the soldiers.
>
> (Arthur, *Above All, Courage*, p. 194)

One could argue that, irrespective of the innate advantages accruing to the Argentines – numerically superior, well dug in, possessing a clear field of fire, much of it in daylight – the fighting spirit of their opponents – their high degree of motivation or 'will to win' – went far in compensating for the defenders' otherwise considerable advantages. As Keeble wrote later of the unit's indomitable spirit: 'We had spent our practice training, fusing the individuals together. The fire of war merely tempered that process. We would never have given up. We would have fought to the last man rather than not achieve the mission.' (Arthur, *Above All, Courage*, p. 191). The paras' high morale stemmed from the strong bond of loyalty that existed between all ranks, in considerable contrast to the weak links known to exist between officers and other ranks in the Argentine army.

Misallocation of Time

While Jones allocated a comfortable period of time in which to allow A Company to plan for the attack on Burntside House (nearly nine hours passed between the end of the 'O' group and Farrar-Hockley leaving the start line), in so doing, he left only four and a half hours for the actual process of fighting to take the company all the way to the outskirts of Darwin and Goose Green. In short, Jones had fourteen hours of darkness, out of which he allocated only a third of that time for by the far the most difficult, time-consuming portion of the operation – the fighting itself. This constituted a very narrow window indeed in which to achieve a great deal. In retrospect, H-Hour ought to have taken place at midnight – or even before – instead of at 0200 hrs. Jones knew very well, but did not seem to account for the fact, that maintaining company cohesion posed difficulties in darkness; fortunately for his men, the Argentines did not put up the level of resistance expected.

Jones had established too optimistic a schedule to meet 2 Para's objective. Had all proceeded according to plan, Darwin Ridge

Lt Col Jones' 'O' group at Camilla Creek House prior to the action. Although he mistakenly believed Coronation Point to be occupied, the intelligence supplied by patrols provided a reasonably accurate picture of Argentine dispositions. His over-optimistic assumption, expressed at the 'O' group, that the defenders would not offer determined resistance, proved false. (Dr Stephen Hughes)

Evacuation of British wounded after the battle. Some casualties had to wait for hours before reaching the RAP or, better still, the medical facility at Ajax Bay, but it is a testament to the high standard of the medics that every man evacuated alive from the field survived the war.

would have been taken before dawn, enabling the assault on the enemy's position to begin within charging distance before the defenders were even aware of the British approach. In the event, Manresa's resistance held up the advance, thus obliging 2 Para to confront the main defensive position in the full glare of daylight. Against more determined opponents, it is unlikely that the British would have succeeded under such disadvantageous circumstances. As Middlebrook rightly concludes: 'Able to see their enemy, to open fire at long range over bare ground, even the reluctant conscripts had the confidence to keep shooting from bunkers and trenches they had had several weeks to prepare.' (Middlebrook, *The Falklands War*, p. 198)

Argentine Inertia and Failure to Counter-attack

The fact that some of Piaggi's troops simply refused to fight – curling up in their sleeping bags or otherwise cowering in the bottom of their trenches in an extraordinary display of passivity – betrayed the gross inexperience and poor discipline in the Argentine army's methods of training. This is not to assert that resistance simply melted away; that was palpably not the case, especially in light of the very fierce resistance offered against C Company's advance on the airfield at midday. But the fact remains that the Argentine army suffered from systemic problems resulting from the highly defective practice of a form of conscription, which, after rudimentary training, released from service the entire year's intake of recruits. This left only the NCOs and officers as a professional cadre, with over-reliance placed on the capabilities of reservists who, in the event, did not arrive in sufficient numbers to replace soldiers only four months into their training.

Moreover, the Argentines demonstrated poor initiative in terms of deploying reinforcements, possibly missing the opportunity to slow 2 Para's progress at the least, or to turn the tide of battle at most. The British stood most vulnerable at dawn – yet encountered no initiative on the part of their opponents. True, the Argentines

Mount Harriet, with a rusted Argentine 105mm recoilless rifle still in situ thirty years later. (Author)

Debris left after the fighting on Mount Longdon. After the war a specialist disposal unit of the Royal Engineers made safe and cleared away vast amounts of weapons and ordnance.

dispatched reinforcements by helicopter to bolster Piaggi's faltering defence, but therein lay the problem: too little, too late. The Argentines could be excused for thinking that Goose Green represented a sort of backwater, never to attract the attention of the Task Force, which all reckoned would land near Stanley. But once the landings took place on 21 May, Menendez and Parada still failed to reinforce Piaggi despite the now realistic prospect that, if only to secure their southern flank, Thompson would attack Goose Green. Menendez possessed plenty of infantry in Stanley and could afford to redeploy a regiment, together with its support weapons, for Piaggi's use, thereby altering entirely the strength of his position on an isthmus too large to accommodate the all-round defence which Parada insisted that Piaggi maintain.

At Goose Green itself, Piaggi failed to profit from the deadlock his defensive line had achieved by counter-attacking at dawn, when A Company stood pinned in front of Darwin Hill and B Company stood deadlocked before Boca House. In short, the Argentines missed their best opportunity to clinch victory from the jaws of defeat.

Inadequate Co-ordination of Fire Support and Absence of an All-arms Approach

2 Para was set the wholly unreasonable objective of defeating an entrenched enemy, established in depth and deployed on a narrow front with clear fields of fire, with no possibility of achieving surprise, virtually no chance of outflanking Piaggi and, perhaps most unforgiveable of all, lacking anything approaching adequate fire support. The fact that HMS *Arrow* experienced technical difficulties with her main gun one may simply attribute to the vagaries of war: Clausewitzian 'friction' or 'Sod's Law', and doubtless gunners and technicians did everything they could – albeit, as it transpired, unsuccessfully – to render their weapon operational. But the absence of adequate artillery support in the field is less forgivable, notwithstanding the critical loss of heavy-lift helicopters on 25 May, when the error of loading so many vitally important machines on

a single transport vessel exposed poor planning at its worst. As for the absence of air support until the closing phases of the battle, the RAF bore no responsibility for this. With better weather on the 27th, Harrier air strikes launched against the isthmus at Jones' request might have accomplished much of the work before 2 Para even left its start line early the following morning, even bearing in mind the presence of anti-aircraft guns, which had already proved their worth in downing two Harriers before the battle. Not until 1530 hrs did three Harriers appear over the battlefield, only one of which managed to strike the peninsula east of Goose Green, but failed to hit the 35mm guns situated there. Still, their presence may have contributed to the Argentines' decision to surrender the following morning.

Yet if one may fairly account for the lack of naval gunfire or air support, the woeful lack of artillery support bears less understanding, with just three 105mm guns available; so few, in fact, that they continually shifted their fire from one company to the next as required. This meant, for example, that although B Company needed

A Royal Artillery gun position, masked with overhead camouflage netting. Only three were present to support 2 Para at Goose Green – a woefully inadequate complement given the difficult task ahead. At the very least, Jones needed more guns which, combined if possible with naval fire support and air cover, would have neutralised Argentine defences in very short order.

fire support during its advance on Boca House, it denied A Company the same support Farrar-Hockley required to break the deadlock in his sector to the east, which came at almost precisely the same time: 1200 hrs. The artillery also expended a considerable amount of ammunition in a wasted effort at counter-battery fire, when lack of intelligence on the location of the Argentine guns rendered this effort futile. Priority ought to have gone to supporting the rifle companies, particularly A and B – those whose advance the Argentines most successfully held up. While the guns operated almost continuously during the fourteen-hour struggle – and fired about 900 shells, giving a rate of fire of about one per minute –they failed to provide the weight of fire required to maintain the troops' momentum. In short, a ground attack requires maximum fire support to aid its advance; even, or perhaps especially, the ordinary soldier appreciates the soundness of this principle. 2 Para prevailed notwithstanding, but the level of fire support provided a fortnight later during the assaults on, in particular, Mount Harriet and Wireless Ridge, should have been present at Goose Green. Finally, given the flat nature of the ground, even the soft, soggy, waterlogged peat could support the weight of light tanks, yet the four Scorpions and four Scimitars from 3 Commando Brigade were, astonishingly, not deployed at Goose Green.

Inadequate Transport and Resupply

2 Para ought to have been deployed on Sussex Mountain by helicopter, obviating the need for their carrying Bergans and kit weighing at least 50kg (110lb) and exhausting the men immediately prior to their launching their assault of 28 May. They were already wet from having come ashore into the icy waters of San Carlos and were badly deprived of sleep, having assembled to disembark into their landing craft from *Norland* at 1000 hrs on the 27th. In fact, Jones realised after the march that he had been mistaken in ordering his men to carry such excessive weight. Helicopters could have brought much of this forward when the battalion established itself at Camilla Creek House a few days later.

A helicopter at Goose Green. Very few British pilots possessed night-sights or experience in night-flying, further limiting senior commanders' options in a war in which supply, resupply and the movement of troops by helicopter proved fundamentally important to success.

During the battle itself, owing to the lack of transport, mortar bombs were brought forward from the original baseplate position near the battalion RV at Camilla Creek House by means of a captured Land Rover. Heavily laden with bombs on the outward journey, the Land Rover then ferried casualties back, just as helicopters shifted ammunition forward and collected the wounded on their return journey. Yet much of the carrying fell upon the backs and shoulders of the Defence Platoon, the Assault Pioneer Platoon and much of the Mortar Platoon – in all sixty men allocated to manual resupply and casevac duties – and therefore not in the frontline. This *ad hoc* method of transport revealed the completely inadequate nature of 2 Para's supply system. It was a mistake for the battalion's Land Rovers to be left on board ship, for without them it would have been impossible to shift mortar bombs forward down what constituted a long battlefield, had not an enemy Land Rover fortuitously fallen into their possession. Gazelles and Sea Kings might have served this function, but they were not intended to fly at night and thus were not in a position to serve this function – and yet the British deliberately planned a night action. Even in daylight, when 2 Para had support from two Scouts and two Gazelles, this amount of lift, largely carrying forward supplies and returning with casualties, proved inadequate. Again, the paras prevailed in spite of insufficient numbers of helicopters – hardly reasonable conditions under which to send men into battle.

Faulty Command Style

Goose Green bears studying for the lessons derived from the inadequacies of Jones' style of command, which dictated orders in so restrictive a form – and to whose strict adherence Jones demanded of his subordinates – that it accounted for his own personal intervention in the frontline and subsequent death, an act of undoubted bravery but the necessity of which continues to fuel controversy today, inside and outside the British Army.

The problem arose from Jones' overly complicated – indeed, almost impossibly complex – six-phase, night/day, silent/noisy attack. His company commanders were required to adhere scrupulously to his plan to enable Darwin and Goose Green to fall before dawn on 28 May, and thus benefit 2 Para from the protection offered by darkness as it advanced over open ground against entrenched defenders. Yet this constituted a hopelessly optimistic timetable, and by imposing a restrictive form of command instead of applying the principle of Mission Command, Jones severely limited the independent action of his subordinates, who ought to have enjoyed the freedom to carry out the CO's intent without the constraints imposed on them as outlined inadequately at his 'O' group. The principle of Mission Command operates on the basis that the overall commander sets out his intent to his subordinates but does not dictate the manner in which they ought to achieve the objective.

While responsibility for the plan continues to rest with the CO – and this applies to junior as well as senior officers – the form in which a subordinate executes that plan rests on the shoulders of, in the case of Goose Green, the company commanders.

The principle does not function well – indeed, can in fact function disastrously – amongst officers ill-equipped to

Members of 2 Para searching prisoners in the streets of Stanley, 14 June.

'appreciate' ground or demonstrate 'situational awareness' (to cite Army terminology), but that could not have been said of 2 Para's company commanders. The process enables commanders to think independently and provides a great degree of flexibility, so enabling them to react rapidly to a fluid situation as they see fit. As a form of decentralisation, Mission Command offers both speed and flexibility of action, and encourages a strong degree of initiative within certain constraints. By imposing a restrictive form of command at Goose Green, Jones at least partly hamstrung his company commanders and, in the case of A Company's stalled attack, contributed to the circumstances that demanded, in his view, his personal presence on the frontline. It also delayed any progress that A Company might have made without his personal intervention, for Jones spent sixty minutes in dead ground in the gorse gully considering his next move, even, unaccountably, refusing to call up Support Company's heavy weapons.

Restrictive command constrains the actions available to a commander if, or rather when, circumstances change and original orders are rendered obsolete, being no longer relevant to developments on the battlefield. For the inexperienced commander, restrictive command offers a number of advantages; but the moment he feels obliged by altered circumstances – and one must bow to the wisdom of von Moltke, who declared that one's plan never survives first contact with the enemy – to refer back to his superior in search of revised orders, precious time, initiative and momentum are lost. If commanding officers had been left to carry out their CO's intent according to their own judgement as circumstances unfolded, one may reasonably argue that Jones need never have made an appearance on Darwin Hill.

Inadequate Numbers, Composition and Disposition of Defenders

The Argentines' chief error in terms of disposition lay in their failure to place troops on Darwin Hill, closing a gap in their otherwise continuous line of defences which might have halted A Company's attack altogether. This constituted a fatal flaw and allowed Farrar-Hockley to approach the gorse gully under considerably less fire than otherwise. Further, Piaggi should never have been ordered to alter his line of defence on the 27th, for by moving Manresa's A Company forward he lost much of the former protection offered by the main defensive line west of Darwin, in whose trenches now stood a mere scratch platoon under Pelufo – a lieutenant with very little experience.

In numerical terms, the Argentines only enjoyed superiority on paper, since both combatants deployed eleven rifle platoons each on 27–28 May. The fact that Piaggi and his air force counterpart commanded together approximately 1,000 personnel (later increased to 1,200) did not reflect the true disparity in numerical strength between the two sides, since many of Piaggi's forces consisted of air force personnel: ground crews and anti-aircraft gunners who could not serve as infantry, plus administrative troops equally inadequate to the task. Lacking sufficient infantry, Piaggi found himself in an unenviable position, for he simply could not defend every possible avenue of approach. He was right to

An Argentine soldier carrying a submachine-gun.

establish a defensive position north of Goose Green; specifically, building a line of trenches on the forward slope and on the crest of the ridge west of Darwin. But he failed to occupy Darwin Hill, a position which controlled both settlements, the airfield and its approaches. At a minimum, he should have occupied the hill with at least a platoon, if not a company – with almost certainly very different consequences to the battle had he done so.

Even the main defensive line proved inadequate, offering no depth on account of trenches dug almost entirely in ordered lines, so leaving platoons unable to support each other with fire. Moreover, the minefield to their front was established too far forward, and thus an attacker could approach and clear a path through the mines without sustaining enemy fire while doing so. Piaggi had also neglected to order the erection of barbed wire in front of the trenches. This alone might have held up 2 Para's progress for a considerable period, or possibly have halted the attack entirely.

A Final Word

Any level-headed military historian must acknowledge the inherent artificiality of sitting back, years after an event, calmly and dispassionately dissecting a battle, taking care to divide it into more or less logical phases for ease of comprehension, before finally rendering judgement on opportunities missed, mistakes made, the virtues of one commander's decision and the folly of another's – all the while, failing to adequately appreciate the immense pressures that rested upon the shoulders of combatants, whose experiences they did not share. Yet the historian brings to bear a perspective not enjoyed by the ordinary soldier or local commander on the ground: a wide perspective on events, which, together with the calm, controlled atmosphere denied participants on the battlefield, furnishes the careful analyst with the tools required to reach at least a modicum of sensible conclusions about the conduct of an engagement.

3 Para advances into Stanley in the wake of their victory at Mount Longdon. Note how they have replaced helmets with their coveted maroon berets.

What, therefore, may be said with some degree of perspective about Goose Green? First, it constituted a remarkable achievement by 2 Para, which overcame a series of prepared defences, in the clear light of day, with virtually no support from other arms. The objectives detailed in the plan of attack were sound, even if the timings were not. Ammunition resupply proved poor, support weapons woefully short in number, naval gunfire and air support virtually non-existent. Yet in spite of this, and in spite of the battalion losing its commanding officer, it prevailed. Even when one accounts for the approximate parity of the rifle companies deployed on both sides, the Argentines still enjoyed more than sufficient advantages with which to mount a successful defence. In the end, the outcome rested firmly with the superior training, discipline and fitness of the paras, backed by exceptionally strong leadership at all levels up the chain of command from section leader to battalion commander. The decisions made, and the conduct displayed, by Lt Col Jones were then, and continue to this day, to be the object of much criticism and controversy. Yet when all is said and done it is difficult to conclude anything other than the ethos which he imbued in the battalion played a decisive part in 2 Para's victory at Goose Green.

ORDERS OF BATTLE

Argentine forces

Task Force Mercedes formed part of 3 Brigade under Brig. Parada who was at Stanley on 28 May. Approx 1,000 ground and air force personnel were commanded by Lt Col Piaggi and Commodore Wilson Pedroza, respectively, later reinforced by approx 200 men.

12th Regiment (excluding B Company, detached to strategic reserve near Mount Kent)

HQ Company

A Company (two platoons): 1st Lt Jorge Manresa (one platoon detached to Stanley); Admin Platoon under 2nd Lt Pelufo (attached to A Company during the battle)

C Company (three platoons): 1st Lt Ramon Fernandez (c. 150 men)

Reconnaissance Platoon (c. 30 men): Lt Carlos Morales (independent of the rifle companies)

Platoon from C Company, 8th Regiment (detached from Fox Bay and attached to A Company, 12th Regiment during the battle): 2nd Lt Guillermo Aliaga

C Company, 25th Regiment (two platoons): 1st Lt Estoban (c. 100 men; one platoon detached to Stanley)

c. 202 Air force ground personnel and AA gunners: Vice-Commodore Pedrosa

> 3 x 105mm pack howitzers
> 2 x 81mm mortars

1 x 120mm mortar
1 x 105mm recoilless rifle (anti-tank)
c. 12 x light machine-guns
2 x 35mm Oerlikon anti-aircraft guns
2 x 20mm Rheinmetall anti-aircraft guns
10 Coast Guard personnel
One section 9th Engineer Company
Mortars: 1 x 120mm; 4 x 81mm (two Army, two Air Force)

Reinforcements (c. 200 personnel)

At approx 1130 hrs 1st Lt Estoban arrived from Stanley with two platoons; c. 100 men in total:

3 Platoon, A Company, 12th Regiment
9 Platoon, C Company, 25th Regiment

At approx 1630 hrs Capt. Corsiglia arrived from Mount Kent with:
B Company, 12th Regiment; c. 100 personnel

British Forces

2 Para Battle Group (Lt Col 'H' Jones); c. 690 personnel, including all attachments:
Battalion HQ (56 men)
Headquarters Company (three platoons plus Regimental Aid Post; c. 100 men): Maj. Ryan
A Company (three platoons; c. 90 men): Maj. Dair Farrar-Hockley
B Company (three platoons; c. 90 men): Maj. John Crosland
C (Patrols) Company (two platoons; c. 55 men): Maj. Richard Jenner
D Company (three platoons; c. 90 men): Maj. Philip Neame

Support Company (c. 128 men): Maj. Hugh Jenner
Anti-tank platoon: 3 x Milans
Mortar platoon: 2 x 81mm mortars
Machine Gun platoon: 6 x GPMGs
Assault Pioneer platoon
Sniper section

Artillery: Maj. Rice
3 x 105mm light guns: 8 (Alma) Batttery, 29 Commando Regiment

6 x Blowpipe missile detachments
Recce Platoon furnished by 59 Ind Commando Squadron
Royal Engineers

BIBLIOGRAPHY
AND FURTHER
READING

Adkin, Mark, *Goose Green: A Battle is Fought to be Won* (London: Phoenix, 2000)

Anderson, Duncan, *The Falklands War 1982* (Oxford: Osprey Publishing, 2002)

Arthur, Max, *Above All, Courage: The Eyewitness History of the Falklands War* (London: Phoenix, 2002)

Badsey, Stephen; Havers, Rob and Grove, Mark (eds), *The Falklands Conflict Twenty Years On: Lessons for the Future* (London: Routledge, 2004)

Banks, Tony, *Storming the Falklands: My War and After* (London: Little, Brown, 2012)

Bicheno, Hugh, *Razor's Edge: The Unofficial History of the Falklands War* (London: Phoenix, 2007)

Bilton, Michael and Kosminsky, Peter (eds), *Speaking Out: Untold Stories from the Falklands War* (London: Grafton Books, 1990)

Bound, Graham, *Falkland Islanders at War* (Barnsley: Pen & Sword Military, 2006)

Burns, Jimmy, *The Land that Lost its Heroes: How Argentina Lost the Falklands War* (London: Bloomsbury Publishing, 2002)

Busser, Carlos, *Operación Rosario* (Buenos Aires: Atlantida, 1984)

Clapp, Michael and Southby-Tailyour, Ewan, *Amphibious Assault Falklands* (Barnsley: Leo Cooper, 1996)

Colbeck, Graham, *With 3 Para to the Falklands* (London: Greenhill Books, 2002)

Curtis, Mike, *CQB: Close Quarter Battle* (London: Corgi, 1998)

De La Billière, General Sir Peter, *Looking for Trouble* (London: HarperCollins, 1994)

English, Adrian, 'The Argentine ground forces in the Falklands campaign,' *Jane's Military Review*, 1986, pp. 139–151

Fitz-Gibbon, Spencer, *Not Mentioned in Dispatches: The History and Mythology of the Battle of Goose Green* (Cambridge: Lutterworth Press, 2001)

Fowler, William, *Battle for the Falklands (1): Land Forces* (London: Osprey Publishing, 2002)

Freedman, Lawrence, *The Official History of the Falklands Campaign. Vol. I: The Origins of the Falklands War* (London: Routledge, 2007)

_____, *The Official History of the Falklands Campaign. Vol. II: War and Diplomacy* (London: Routledge, 2007)

_____, *Signals of War: The Falklands Conflict of 1982* (Princeton: Princeton University Press, 1992)

Fremont-Barnes, Gregory, *Falklands 1982: Ground Operations in the South Atlantic* (Oxford: Osprey Publishing, 2012)

Frost, Major General John, *2 Para in the Falklands: The Battalion at War* (London: Buchan & Enright, 1983)

Geddes, John, *Spearhead Assault: Blood, Guts and Glory on the Falklands Frontlines* (London: Arrow Books, 2008)

Hastings, Max and Jenkins, Simon, *The Battle for the Falklands* (London: Pan, 2010)

Hilton, Christopher, *Ordinary Heroes: Untold Stories from the Falklands Campaign* (Stroud: The History Press, 2012)

Informe oficial del Ejército Argentino: conflicto Malvinas. [Official Report of the Argentine army: the Malvinas conflict], 2 vols. (Buenos Aires: *Ejército Argentino*, 1983)

Jolly, Rick, *Doctor for Friend and Foe: Britain's Frontline Medic in the Fight for the Falklands* (London: Conway, 2012)

Kenney, David, *2 Para's Battle for Darwin Hill and Goose Green* (Oak Square Press, 2006)

McManners, Hugh (ed.), *Forgotten Voices of the Falklands: The Real Story of the Falklands War* (London: Ebury Press, 2008)

Middlebrook, Martin, *Argentine Fight for the Falklands* (Barnsley: Pen & Sword Military, 2009)

_____, *The Falklands War 1982* (London: Penguin Classics, 2007)

Middleton, J.D., *et al*, *The Falkland Islands: Goose Green, Darwin* (Leavenworth: Combat Studies Institute, 1983)

Oakley, Derek, *The Falklands Military Machine* (Stroud: The History Press, 2002)

Orgill, Andrew, *The Falklands War: Background, Conflict, Aftermath* (London: Continuum, 1993)

Parsons, Michael, *The Falklands War* (Stroud: Sutton Publishing, 2000)

Piaggi, Italo, *El Combate de Goose Green* (Buenos Aires: Planeto, 1994)

Ramsey, Gordon, *The Falklands War Then and Now* (Harlow: Battle of Britain International Ltd, 2009)

Ratcliffe, Peter, *Eye of the Storm* (London: Michael O'Mara Books, 2000)

Smith, Gordon, *Battle Atlas of the Falklands War 1982* (Naval History, 2006)

Thompson, Julian, *3 Commando Brigade in the Falklands: No Picnic* (Barnsley: Pen & Sword Military, 2008)

Van Der Bijl, Nick and Aldea, David, *5th Infantry Brigade in the Falklands* (Barnsley: Pen & Sword, 2002)

Van Der Bijl, Nick, *Argentine Forces in the Falklands* (Oxford: Osprey Publishing, 2005)

_____, *Nine Battles to Stanley* (Barnsley: Leo Cooper, 1999)

_____, *Victory in the Falklands* (Barnsley: Pen & Sword Military, 2007)

Vaux, Nick, *March to the South Atlantic* (London: Buchan and Enright, 1986)

Watson, Bruce and Dunn, Peter, *Military Lessons of the Falkland Islands War* (London: Arms & Armour Press, 1984)

Wilsey, John, *H Jones VC: The Life and Death of an Unusual Hero* (London: Hutchinson, 2000)

Woodward, Sandy, with Robinson, Patrick, *One Hundred Days: The Memoirs of the Falklands Battle Group Commander* (London: HarperCollins; 2010)

INDEX